Quebec

BIRTHPLACE OF NEW FRANCE

DAVID MENDEL

PHOTOGRAPHS
LUC-ANTOINE COUTURIER

DESIGN
ANDRÉ DUROCHER

A VISUAL EXPLORATION OF QUEBEC CITY

This book is the second in a series of four volumes that will provide a visual exploration of Quebec City, its history and its architecture. While the first volume, **Quebec, World Heritage City,** focused on the upper town, this one, **Quebec, Birthplace of New France,** takes us down to the lower town, where the city began early in the 17th century with the establishment of a little trading post by the shore of the St. Lawrence River. The evolution of the lower town has always been tied to the rising and falling fortunes of Quebec as a maritime city. Over the centuries, the needs of the port determined not only the size and scale of the buildings in the sector, but even the amount of land available for construction.

A brief outline of the history of each major location leads to a step-by-step exploration, in which general exterior and interior views are followed by photographs of selected objects, symbols and architectural elements. Texts have been kept deliberately short in order to provide as much space as possible for historic maps, images and, especially, Luc-Antoine Couturier's remarkable photographs. As we will see, a wide variety of historic buildings and structures have survived in the lower town. Evidence of Quebec's evolution as a port city remains visible at almost every corner, waiting to be discovered by the observant eye. It is a story that is told in brick and stone.

QUEBEC

BIRTHPLACE OF NEW FRANCE

The destiny of Quebec, founded by French explorer Samuel de Champlain in 1608, has always been tied to the city's remarkable strategic location. The "Key to the Continent", Quebec is situated at the head of the St. Lawrence estuary, where the river suddenly narrows to a width of only one kilometre. Here, from the natural fortress of *Cap-aux-Diamants*, 17th-century cannons could bar the passage of enemy ships. At first a small trading post, Quebec became the capital of New France, a fortress city, commanding the gateway between the Atlantic World and the interior of the continent.

CHAMPLAIN'S TRADING POST

Samuel de Champlain first sailed up the St. Lawrence estuary as a member of a French expedition in 1603. At Tadoussac, where the Saguenay River enters the St. Lawrence, the explorers met with the Innu, a nomadic Algonquin-speaking peo-ple who claimed control of the region. The Innu invited the French to join them in a commercial and military alliance. In return for taking up arms with the Innu against their enemies the Iroquois, the French were given permission to set up a trading post further inland. In 1608, Champlain chose a site on the shore of the St. Lawrence River known as Quebec, a name that has its origin with a word in an Algonquin language meaning "where the river narrows". By establishing themselves at this natural control point Champlain and his men hoped to be able to stop rival Basque and the Dutch fur traders from having access to the continental interior. Moreover, by joining forces with the Innu, the French would be able to benefit from their trading alliances with other Amerindian peoples further inland: Algonquian-speaking groups and Hurons, whose trade routes along the rivers led to the richest sources of furs.

During their first years here, Champlain and his men chose to leave their large ships at Tadoussac. Having little knowledge of the St. Lawrence River, which can be extremely difficult to navigate, they travelled up the estuary to Quebec in smaller, shallow-draught boats. By the 1630s, however, French transatlantic ships were sailing inland all the way to Quebec. Beyond that point the river became too difficult to navigate. The large ships were thus obliged to stop at Quebec to unload their cargoes.

GATEWAY TO A CONTINENT

In 1663, Louis XIV chose the strategic site of Quebec to establish the capital of New France. This fortified city and inland seaport - hundreds of kilometres from the Atlantic - would serve as a control point between the Atlantic World and the vast network of navigable rivers and lakes that would become the lifeblood of the French empire in North America. The basin before Quebec City provided water deep enough for the largest warships and merchant vessels to safely drop anchor. Beyond Quebec, smaller, shallow draught-boats were able to navigate upriver until their passage was blocked at Montreal by the Lachine rapids. Travel beyond that point was easiest by birch-bark canoe.

French expansion - along the St. Lawrence, to the Ottawa River and the Great Lakes, then down the Mississippi to the Gulf of Mexico - has been compared to the growth of the branches of a tree. Forts and trading posts were established along the main rivers and then their principal tributaries, providing access ever deeper into the hinterland. Many North American cities that we think of today as being English, began as French forts and trading posts: *Fort Toronto* is now Toronto, Ontario; *Fort Frontenac* is now Kingston, Ontario; *Détroit* is now Detroit, Michigan; and *La Nouvelle Orléans* is now New Orleans, Louisiana.

At first Quebec's little lower town was confined to the area where the Place Royale sector is today. Elsewhere, the shore was submerged at high tide. In order to provide more land surface for construction, the mudflats shown in this 18th-century map were gradually covered over. By the end of the 19th century, the lower town had doubled in size.

CONTRASTING PATTERNS OF SETTLEMENT

In contrast to the French, who had penetrated deep into the North American interior by the late 1600s, their principal competitors, the English, unable to expand into the West because they were blocked by New France, remained hemmed in along a narrow band of land between the Atlantic Ocean and the Appalachian Mountains. But while the English territories along the Atlantic seaboard did not allow much room for expansion, they did offer some important advantages. With ice-free seaports providing access to the Atlantic twelve months a year, and rich land for agriculture, the English population grew rapidly. The first English settlement, Jamestown (founded in 1607, one year before Quebec City), soon developed a thriving economy based on the export of tobacco. But large-scale agriculture quickly brought the English into conflict with the native peoples, leading to the

first of a long series of bloody confrontations that would characterize English expansion along the North American frontier.

ALLIANCES WITH THE NATIVE PEOPLES: THE KEY TO FRENCH POWER

The French, on the other hand, were much more interested in doing business with the native peoples than in taking over their lands in the interior regions. Most of the French population was concentrated in the St. Lawrence lowlands, which provided enough good agricultural land for the colony of New France, with its economy based mainly on the fur trade. Beyond the St. Lawrence Valley, in the vast territories that they referred to as *le pays d'en haut*, the French never became numerous enough to impose their will on the native peoples. Instead, French policy sought, as often as possible,

Native groups began to frequent the site of Quebec at least 3000 years ago. This early 19ᵗʰ-century watercolour depicts a Micmac encampment on the south shore of the St. Lawrence, across the river from the city.

to establish commercial and military alliances with the Amerindian nations. Indeed, the arrival of settlers in the continental interior would have been disastrous for the fur trade. Settlers would have cut down the trees and pushed the animals out of the way, just as they would have driven away the native hunters and trappers upon whom the French fur-traders depended for their livelihood.

Pressures were mounting. By the mid 18ᵗʰ century there were over one and a half million English-speaking people squeezed into the narrow band of land along the Atlantic coast, facing a French population of only about 60,000 to defend the entire continental interior. The English colonies, bursting at the seams, were becoming a serious threat, both to the inland empire of New France and to the native way of life. Recognizing this danger, an increasing number of native groups chose to actually invite the French to establish forts and trading posts on their territories to help serve as

a barrier to English expansion. Without the help of the native peoples, it would have been impossible for the French, with such small numbers, to exert their influence over the interior of the continent for as long as they did.

THE FALL OF NEW FRANCE

Finally, however, New France was conquered by the English. In 1763, with the Treaty of Paris, the regions to the west of the Appalachians officially became English territory. Only decades later, following the American Revolution, hundreds of thousands of settlers would pour over the Appalachians and the native tribes would be swept away. It would only be a matter of time before the fur trade started to decline as well, as the natural environment on which it had depended began to disappear.

FROM FURS TO WOOD

During the last decades of the 18th century, the economy of Quebec City was still based on the fur trade and any changes in the port area tended to be slow and gradual. At the beginning of the 19th century, however, international events would give new importance to the port of Quebec, leading to major transformations in the lower town. During the Napoleonic Wars, France cut England off from its traditional sources of wood in the Baltic region. The British then looked to the forests of Canada for new supplies, and the port of Quebec experienced a period of remarkable economic expansion. Fortunes were made here as Britain's need for wood, and wooden ships, transformed this little colonial city into one of the greatest ports in North America. Between 1806 and 1814, wood exports from the port of Quebec increased from 100,000 to 370,000 tonnes. And that was just the beginning. A comparison of the number of ships entering the port over the years can give us an idea of the extraordinary increase in activity in the port of Quebec during this period. While during the 18th century a maximum of 80 transatlantic ships had visited the port each year, by 1811 the number had risen to 188 vessels. By the 1860s, between 1500 and 1700 ships were docking at Quebec City annually. Shipbuilding became big business. The number of ships constructed at Quebec rose from only 7 in the year 1800 to an average of 49 ships annually by 1850.

ONE OF THE WORLD'S GREAT PORTS

By the middle of the 19th century, Quebec City was doing more business than the port of Boston, and only New York City and New Orleans handled more tonnes of cargo. Quebec also became one of the most important ports for immigration from the British Isles to North America. Ships that were used to transport wood to Great Britain returned to Quebec City with a poverty stricken human ballast of English, Scottish and Irish immigrants hoping for a better life in the New World. By the 1830s an average of 30,000 people were disembarking in Quebec City annually. At the time of the great famine in Ireland, in 1847, almost 90,000 people landed on the docks of Quebec - this at a time when the permanent population of the city was only about 45,000! In that year, only New York City received more Irish immigrants than Quebec. Most of these immigrants continued on to other destinations further west, or in the United States,

but the pressures on Quebec City must have been enormous. The upper town offered some room for expansion but the port area quickly became built up and solutions had to be found to compensate for the limited land surface that was available. Land reclamation efforts that had begun slowly during the French regime were accelerated to meet the needs of the expanding port, and by the end of the 19th century the lower town had doubled in size.

THE LOWER TOWN EVOLVES WITH THE PORT

During the 17th and 18th centuries, minimal port facilities had been required to export furs and receive supplies for the small population of the colony. Indeed, until the end of the 17th century the city did not have any docks at all. Large sailing ships were obliged to anchor out in deep water, where small boats went out to meet them to load and unload their cargoes. The little boats were simply beached on the shore. Wooden enclosures were constructed along the shoreline, to protect the labourers handling the cargoes from the waves of the St. Lawrence and the rising tide. At the turn of the 18th century, these wooden structures were replaced by stone walls equipped with iron mooring rings to allow boats to tie up alongside at high tide. Although these stone quays served as docking facilities, they were not located in water deep enough to accommodate large vessels. In the early 19th century, individual property owners began to construct long wooden wharves, projecting out into deep water so that big ships could dock directly beside them, even at low tide. These structures reached out into the river like a series of long fingers, with each wharf named after its owner: Grant's Wharf, Hunt's Wharf, etc. To provide storage space for the greater volume of cargo now being handled in the port, large warehouses, called "stores," were constructed on the merchant's private wharves. A good example of one of these early "stores" is the Chillas warehouse, built in 1822, which is now part of the Auberge St. Antoine. Toward the end of the 19th century much bigger warehouses were being constructed. On nearby *Rue Saint Pierre* other large buildings were constructed to house banks and other enterprises that served the needs of the growing port.

During the first decades of the 19th century, well-to-do merchants continued to reside in the port area, despite the increasing noise and activity.

ABOVE: This romantic view, painted by George Heriot, depicts sleighs gliding over the frozen St. Charles River in 1805, with Quebec City in the background. – BELOW: In the 19th century it was no easy task to transport passengers and the mail over the icy waters of the St. Lawrence River. Today, an ice canoe race, held each year during the Quebec Winter Carnival, evokes the days when this strenuous activity was a necessity rather than a sport.

However, when in the 1830s and 1840s immigrants arrived bringing cholera and typhus which killed thousands of local citizens, the merchants began to move away from the lower town. Many established themselves in the upper town, or built villas in the countryside, to move their families as far as possible from the port, where deadly diseases arrived with the ships. This was the beginning of a gradual reorganization of the city into business, manufacturing and residential districts.

THE SEASONS, THE WINDS AND THE TIDES

In the days of sail, almost every aspect of life in Quebec was affected in some way by the town's relationship with the water. Visitors arrived by ship, as did correspondence and news from afar. Most people depended on the river for their employment. They found jobs in the fur trade, ship-building, the timber trade and the many other businesses related to the life of the port. Many activities had to be scheduled in relation to the

realities of river life - the seasons, the winds and the tides. For example, sailing vessels had to time their arrivals and departures to take advantage of favourable winds. They used the rising tide to go inland and the falling tide to head out to sea. Farmers travelled by boat to deliver their produce and firewood to riverside markets, such as the *Marché Champlain*, seen in this photograph (*below*), taken around 1880. Animals were slaughtered on the Island of Orleans at the beginning of winter, so that the frozen meat could be delivered to market by sleigh over the frozen river, via the "ice bridge". The river was shallow enough between the island and the north shore to ensure that it would freeze solid each winter. In front of the city, however, the St. Lawrence is much deeper and an ice bridge could only form when the weather was particularly cold. When the river was not completely frozen, boatmen hired their services to transport passengers and goods across the river - over and between the moving ice floes - no easy undertaking (*see page 13*). In ways that are hard for us to imagine today, Quebec was truly a maritime city.

DECLINE... AND RENAISSANCE

Quebec's time of prosperity and expansion as a great 19th century port city, however, was to be short-lived. By mid-century, a shipping channel had been dug in the St. Lawrence, deep enough to allow the passage of transatlantic vessels all the way to Montreal. Quebec thus lost its exclusive status as a great inland seaport linking the Atlantic Ocean with the western interior. A new era of iron, steel and steam sounded the death knell of the age of sail. Steam-powered vessels could now navigate the shipping channel up the St. Lawrence to Montreal much more easily than sailing ships, which were dependent on the changing winds. Railways now made it possible to bypass the ice-filled river in wintertime, connecting Montreal with an ice-free port in Portland Maine, while the port of Quebec was stuck in the ice.

British preferential tariffs that had protected the timber trade were abolished and wood exports from the port of Quebec plummeted. Then, when the British began to build metal ships at home, the market for the wooden ships constructed at Quebec collapsed completely. By the turn of the century, many workers who had lost their jobs in the port were looking for new employment in the factories of the St. Roch district or had left Quebec City altogether to seek work.

Great efforts would be required to revive the fortunes of Quebec's port. The harbour was dredged and more deep-water docking facilities were constructed at the mouth of the St. Charles River, where a grain terminal was established by the *Bassin Louise*. Much of the development, however,

would take place far from the original lower town, as the port expanded along the shoreline to *Anse-au-Foulon* in the 1930s, and on the *Battures de Beauport* in the 1960s. As a result, the old port and business sectors were gradually abandoned and many buildings in the lower town were demolished or left to deteriorate.

With cars and highways dominating daily life, and access to the dock areas forbidden, most local citizens lost touch with their maritime heritage. Then, in 1984, the waterfront was opened up to the public, with fine brick-paved promenades beside new deep-water docking facilities, where cruise ship passengers could step out directly into Quebec's historic waterfront sector. In the years that followed, the lower town experienced a renaissance,

with the opening of the *Musée de la civilisation*, in 1988, the conversion of old warehouses for residential use, and the establishment of fine boutique hotels, shops and restaurants.

The port as a whole, now accessible in winter thanks to ice-breakers, has undergone a renaissance as well. Today, as vessels become ever larger, Quebec's natural deep-water port offers considerable advantages once more. With expanded facilities able to accommodate Panamax and even Capesize vessels, which can carry cargoes of as much as 150,000 tonnes, Quebec City has been able to reaffirm its traditional role as a great inland seaport, providing a deepwater connection to the Great Lakes and the interior of North America.

OLD POST OFFICE

AN IMPOSING EDIFICE

The old Post Office is one of the most imposing buildings in Quebec's historic district. Constructed in 1871 according to the plans of architect Pierre Gauvreau, then enlarged in 1913, the Post Office was re-named in 1984 to honour the memory of one of the city's most distinguished citizens, Louis S. St. Laurent, prime minister of Canada from 1949 to 1958. Although the building no longer serves as the city's central post office, it still provides postal services for customers in Quebec's upper town. Today, most of the build-

ing is occupied by the regional offices of Parks Canada. The 1913 enlargement, which greatly enhanced the dignity of the edifice, is crowned by a monumental copper-roofed dome, seen here on a winter's night from a room in the nearby Chateau Frontenac hotel.

The same enlargement included a new façade, graced by massive columns and a triangular pediment, facing *Côte de la Montagne*. Although somewhat difficult to see from the streets below, the new additions made the building very impressive when seen from a distance – especially for visitors arriving by ship (*see page 21*). Prior to the construction of the Post Office building in 1871, the site was occupied by one of the city's largest 18th-century houses. Known as *le Chien d'Or*, the old stone house (*see next page*) had first served as a private residence, then as an inn, as a Masonic Hall and as a post office, before being finally demolished to make way for the present edifice.

THE GOLDEN DOG

Prominently displayed over the portico of the Louis S. St-Laurent building is an ancient stone plaque (*above*). For generations this plaque was located over the entrance door of *le Chien d'Or*. Beneath a relief sculpture of a golden dog is a text in old French which, translated into English, reads:

I am a dog that gnaws his bone,
I crouch and gnaw it all alone.
A time will come, which is not yet,
When I'll bite him by whom I'm bit.

In 1748, the merchant who owned the house, Nicolas Jacquin dit Philibert, was murdered by Le Gardeur de Repentigny, a military officer from a distinguished Quebec family. Although the plaque is dated 1736 – twelve years before Philibert's death – the mysterious words inscribed in the stone quickly became associated with the story of his murder. Generations of Quebec citizens exchanged fanciful tales about the crime. The legend eventually inspired William Kirby to write a popular 19th-century novel of revenge and murder, entitled The Golden Dog.

AN IMPRESSIVE ENTRANCE TO THE UPPER TOWN

At the beginning of the 20th century, plans were developed to create an impressive new entrance to the upper town for people arriving from the lower town via the *Côte de la Montagne*. More stone houses at the top of the hill were demolished – with little concern for their historic value – to make way for a statue of the first bishop of Quebec, François de Laval (*see next chapter*). A new public square was laid out, with wide, curving stairways flanking the monument. In addition to creating a worthy setting for the statue of the bishop, the demolitions made it easier to appreciate the imposing architecture of the Post Office building, seen here from a privileged vantage point: the roof of the archbishop's residence (*next pages*).

Fʀᴀɴᴄ̧ᴏɪs ᴅᴇ Lᴀᴠᴀʟ

FIRST BISHOP OF QUEBEC

François de Laval (1623-1708) founded the French Catholic Church in North America. In 1659 he was sent to New France as the Pope's representative, or Vicar Apostolic, and was recognized as the first bishop in 1674. He faced a colossal task. In 1663, to establish a solid foundation for his church in the New World, Laval founded a community of diocesan priests, the *Séminaire de Québec*. Then, in 1688, to provide an education for young boys destined for the priesthood, he founded the *Petit Séminaire de Québec*.

Undaunted by the severe climate and harsh wilderness conditions of his enormous diocese, Laval travelled hundreds of kilometres by snowshoe and canoe to visit the fledgling parishes along the St. Lawrence, where most of the population of the French colony was concentrated. The diocese of Quebec, however, extended far beyond the St. Lawrence valley. The vast territories under Laval's jurisdiction were truly continental in scale – stretching over most of the area that is now occupied by both Canada and the United States.

A stern defender of the spiritual welfare of those under his charge, the first bishop fought long and hard to prevent the sale of alcohol to the native peoples. As *l'eau de vie* was considered of crucial importance for the lucrative fur trade, François de Laval's determined moral stand on alcohol brought him into frequent conflict with the elite of the colony, including the governor.

Created by the renowned sculptor Louis-Philippe Hébert, this impressive monument, erected in 1908 – two hundred years after the bishop's death – honours François de Laval as an evangelist, educator and statesman.

The unveiling of the Laval Monument in 1908 coincided with the 300th anniversary of the founding of Quebec City. The ceremony, with over 50,000 people in attendance, was one of the first major public events of the tri-centennial celebrations. By inaugurating the statue of the first bishop during Quebec's tri-centennial year, the Catholic Church sought to honour François de Laval as a father of French Canada, on the same footing as the founder of the city, Samuel de Champlain.

THE SHEPHERD WHO TENDS HIS FLOCK

Dressed in full episcopal regalia, François de Laval (*preceding pages*) looks down from atop his granite pedestal; his right hand is extended toward us, while his left hand holds the bishop's staff, or crosier – symbolizing the shepherd who tends his flock.

EVANGELIST, EDUCATOR AND STATESMAN

At the base of the monument (*above, left*) are allegorical figures in bronze: To the left, a winged angel, personifying *la patrie* (the nation), offers the first bishop a laurel branch – a symbol of glory – in recognition of his many accomplishments. Beneath *la patrie*, a young student, wearing the uniform of the *Petit Séminaire de Québec*, evokes the bishop's role as an educator.

A feminine figure (*above*) representing Religion, gestures toward the young student. Behind the figure of Religion, a parish church, sculpted in low relief, symbolizes the central role played by François de Laval in establishing the Catholic Church in North America. The bishop's mission to evangelize the native peoples is symbolized by a proud Amerindian. This warrior looks away, expressing, perhaps, the ambivalence that many natives felt about French efforts to convert them to the Catholic religion.

PANELS IN BRONZE RELIEF

On three sides of the granite base, panels in bronze relief depict important moments in the life of François de Laval.

The audience with Louis XIV (*facing page, above*) emphasizes Bishop Laval's prominent role in matters of state and the governing of New France. As

the leader of the Church and a member of the Sovereign Council, François de Laval's powers could sometimes rival those of the governor.

This emphasis on the temporal powers of the first bishop reflected issues that were of great importance to the Catholic Church when this monument was erected. In 1904, France had severed diplomatic ties with the Vatican, and had passed a law in 1905 separating Church and State. Large numbers of French priests and nuns, fleeing their anticlerical government, had crossed the Atlantic to establish themselves in the Province of Quebec. The church authorities of French Canada, who saw themselves as defenders of French-speaking Catholics everywhere, sought to promote the unity of Church and State in the symbolic program of this monument.

The panel on the following pages shows Bishop Laval accompanied by a procession of priests and representatives of the religious orders who helped him spread the faith, establish educational institutions, and care for the poor and sick.

THE BISHOP'S LEGACY

The location selected for the monument ensured that François de Laval's statue would face three important buildings that related to his life and legacy as first bishop of Quebec: the Seminary of Quebec, founded by Bishop Laval in 1663; the impressive residence of the Archbishop of Quebec, constructed to house François de Laval's successors in 1844; and Laval University, founded in 1852 – the first French Catholic university in North America – named by the priests of the Seminary in honour of their founder. Laval's statue also faces Montmorency Park. The first bishop, sometimes referred to as François de Montmorency Laval, was a descendent of one of the most distinguished and aristocratic lineages of France, the Montmorency family.

THE BAPTISM OF GARAKONTIÉ

Garakontié was a highly respected Onandaga chief who played a crucial role in peace negotiations between the French and the Five-Nations Iroquois. This bronze panel depicts the baptism of Garakontié by Bishop Laval in 1670. The native leader's godparents – Daniel de Rémy de Courcelle, Governor General of New France, and Mademoiselle de Boutroue d'Aubigny, the daughter of the Intendant – each place a hand on Garakontié's shoulder.

Native chiefs, who had come to Quebec to participate in the peace negotiations, are depicted on the right-hand side of the panel

(detail, above right). One holds a peace pipe. On the ground, at the feet of the native leaders, lie a hatchet and quiver of arrows, symbolizing an end to war.

Garakontié was an influential orator among the Five-Nations Iroquois. Some chiefs disagreed with his conciliatory approach, however, and others were jealous of him. In Hébert's remarkable character study (detail, above), we can sense their mixed feelings regarding Garakontié's special relationship with the French, and his decision to adopt their religion.

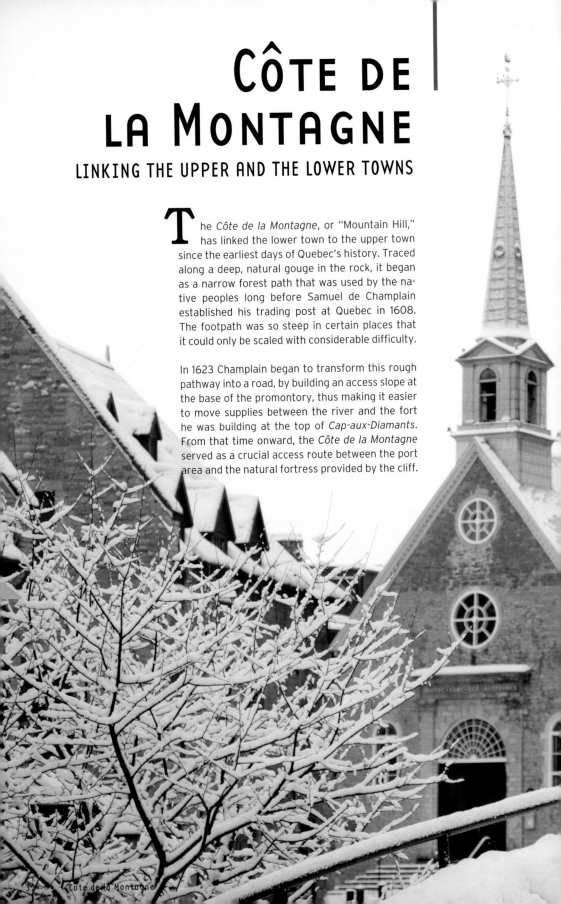

CÔTE DE LA MONTAGNE
LINKING THE UPPER AND THE LOWER TOWNS

The *Côte de la Montagne*, or "Mountain Hill," has linked the lower town to the upper town since the earliest days of Quebec's history. Traced along a deep, natural gouge in the rock, it began as a narrow forest path that was used by the native peoples long before Samuel de Champlain established his trading post at Quebec in 1608. The footpath was so steep in certain places that it could only be scaled with considerable difficulty.

In 1623 Champlain began to transform this rough pathway into a road, by building an access slope at the base of the promontory, thus making it easier to move supplies between the river and the fort he was building at the top of *Cap-aux-Diamants*. From that time onward, the *Côte de la Montagne* served as a crucial access route between the port area and the natural fortress provided by the cliff.

The commercial sector, by the river, provided the city with supplies and revenues from exports, while the upper town - where most of the political and religious institutions were concentrated - assured the city's defence.

Over the centuries, certain professions tended to establish themselves along the *Côte de la Montagne*, to benefit from the specific advantages offered by this transitional zone between the upper and lower towns. For example, in the late 17th century, Governor Frontenac ordered blacksmiths to move to the *Côte de la Montagne*, in an effort to isolate their workshops - where accidental fires might start - from the more densely populated parts of the city. In the 18th century, many suppliers of luxury goods, including jewellers, silversmiths and clockmakers, chose to locate their businesses along this much frequented roadway, where they could serve the elites of both the upper and lower towns. Later, during the 19th and 20th centuries, printers and bookbinders were attracted to the *Côte de la Montagne*, because this location allowed them to be close to their principal clients - the governmental and religious institutions of the upper town - and the banks, import/export businesses, and insurance companies in the port area. In the early 20th century, when the lower town was still the centre of business, many accountants and lawyers had their offices in the lower part of the *Côte de la Montagne*. Today, the street is dominated by restaurants and shops that serve the thousands of tourists who go up and down the hill each day.

THE FIRST CEMETERY

The site of Quebec's first cemetery at nightfall (*preceding page*). In the background, the *Côte de la Montagne* winds down the cliff beneath the dramatic silhouette of the Chateau Frontenac.

Today a red wooden cross marks the site of the first cemetery (*left*). Samuel de Champlain and his men spent a very difficult first winter at Quebec, in 1608-1609. The founder of Quebec began the winter with twenty-eight men, but by the spring, only eight were left. The rest had died of scurvy or dysentery, and were buried on this small plot of ground beside the *Côte de la Montagne*.

TOP LEFT - The road was gradually widened and improved during the 17th and 18th centuries, but it still became so wet and muddy that after a heavy rain it could be almost impassable. This view shows the terrible damage caused by the British bombardments of 1759. The Bishop's Palace (to the centre-left), was constructed in 1693-95. Although damaged by firebombs, the stone building remained solid enough to be converted into the first parliament of Lower Canada in 1791.

TOP MIDDLE - Quebec City's steep cliff was its greatest defence, and military control of the *Côte de la Montagne* was always an important concern, but it was not until 1797 that the Prescott Gate was built to command this crucial access point. With a narrow archway - enabling sentries to control the passage of vehicles one at a time - the gate no doubt served its military function very well, but it must have caused never-ending traffic problems. The Prescott Gate was demolished in 1871, the year the British Army left the city.

TOP RIGHT - A view of the *Côte de la Montagne*, in 1860.

PREVIOUS PAGE BOTTOM - The large stone house in the foreground is the *Maison Garon*, portions of which date back to 1740. After sustaining serious damage during the siege of 1759, the residence was reconstructed in 1766. Two centuries later, in 1966, the appearance of the house was modified considerably. An additional storey was added and the dimensions of the door and window on the ground floor were altered.

BELOW - In 1983, to celebrate Quebec City's 375th anniversary, Parks Canada constructed a new version of the Prescott Gate, which connects the Frontenac stairs with Montmorency Park.

The *Côte de la Montagne*, seen from the ramparts, around 1880. Dominating the scene in the background are the stone-buttressed Dufferin Terrace – a public boardwalk with superb views of the river, which had recently been extended in 1878-79 – and the Citadel of Quebec, the great fortress built by the British between 1820 and 1831.

Joseph Canac *dit* Marquis built this house in 1768, on the foundations of a residence that had been badly damaged during the bombardments of 1759. When seen from the *Côte-de-la-Montagne*, the stone residence appears to be only two and a half storeys high. This photograph, however, taken from a nearby rooftop, reveals an addition, built in 1867, which extends down the cliff to provide four storeys of living space.

The Neptune Inn

For generations, one of the most popular drinking establishments in Quebec City's lower town was the Neptune Inn, located at the foot of the *Côte de la Montagne*, depicted in this watercolour by James Pattison Cockburn in 1830. Above the door is a wooden sculpture of Neptune, the Roman god of the sea. This carving had originally been the figurehead of the Neptune, a king's ship that had run aground on Anticosti Island, at the mouth of the Gulf of St. Lawrence, in 1817. According to 19th-century historian and author James MacPherson Le Moine, many local sailors and dockworkers were convinced that this impressive, bearded figure, watching over a favourite haunt of English sea captains, was Lucifer himself, brandishing his pitchfork.

The Neptune Inn eventually closed and the building was temporarily taken over by newspaper offices in 1875. Then, in 1901, the inn reopened under new ownership. The proprietor engaged one of Quebec's greatest wood sculptors, Louis Jobin, to carve a new statue of the sea god. Jobin's bearded Neptune holds his traditional trident and wears an impressive classical helmet. Notice, however, that the artist chose to give the figure a contemporary touch, by clothing him in the apparel of a modern sailor.

STAIRCASES

Because of the steepness of the cliff, the *Côte de la Montagne* must follow a winding route. Staircases have provided shortcuts for pedestrians ever since the 17th century.

The oldest staircase (*top right*) connects a curve, half way down the *Côte de la Montagne,* with *Rue Petit-Champlain*, in the lower town. While this staircase has been reconstructed many times, it has remained in the same location since the 17th century. Its name, "Breakneck Stairs", refers to a time when it was much steeper and more rickety than it is today. This photograph, taken by Louis-Prudent Vallée around 1870, shows a very animated scene, with crowds of people standing on the stairs below a colourful array of overhead signs to identify the many businesses that lined the "Breakneck Stairs".

This cast-iron staircase (*bottom right*) is named after Charles Baillairgé, the architect and city engineer who designed it in 1893. It was restored by the City of Quebec in 1980.

The Frontenac Stairs (*facing page*) constructed in 1978, link the Dufferin Terrace with the *Côte de la Montagne*.

LA FRESQUE DES QUÉBÉCOIS

A FANCIFUL CITYSCAPE

The *Fresque des Québécois* (Mural of Quebeckers) is a 420-square-metre *trompe-l'oeil* mural painted on a building at the foot of the *Côte de la Montagne*. It is a source of constant fascination for passersby.

"*Trompe-l'oeil*", literally translated, means to fool the eye. Highly skilled artists have transformed a nondescript, blank wall into a marvellous, imaginary cityscape. With consummate artistry, they have created the illusion that the historic buildings and architectural elements depicted in the mural are, in fact, real structures, projecting out toward us as if they were truly three-dimensional. Observe, for example, the false cornices, painted in ochre and green in the upper portion of the mural (*following pages, left and right*). See how cleverly the artists have imitated the appearance of real cornices – just beside them – that truly project from the other sides of the building.

Artists from the French city of Lyon, where there is a strong tradition of *trompe-l'oeil* mural painting, were invited by the *Commission de la capitale nationale du Québec* to work with local artists to create this work of art in 1999. *La Fresque des Québécois* is a fanciful urban landscape, inspired by Quebec's history and architectural heritage.

THE CHANGING SEASONS

Observe how the creators of this work of art have played with the passage of time (*preceding pages*): winter snow covers the roofs of buildings depicted at the top of the mural. Then, as we look downwards, the seasons shift to autumn, to summer and finally to spring. Portraits of famous figures from the city's past are interspersed alongside images of people from the present day (*see following pages*): Louis de Buade, Count Frontenac (*top right*), one of the most famous governors of New France, is depicted holding a scroll. Next to the image of the governor is a depiction of a bearded man, holding a globe (*top left*). This is Jacques Cartier, the first French explorer to come to the site of Quebec, in 1535. At the bottom left is a portrait of an elegant Victorian gentleman who played a key role in the history of the city and the preservation of its architectural heritage. This is Lord Dufferin, the British Governor General who led a campaign to save Quebec's fortification walls from demolition in the 1870s. Beside his portrait, children of today (*bottom right*) are enjoying a game of street hockey. Other figures from the present, including a romantic couple kissing on a city gate, are interspersed among the portraits of great figures from the past. The first *Intendant* (chief administrator) of New France, Jean Talon (*facing page*), seems to look out at us from a painted window. Talon, who served as *Intendant* during the 1660s and 1670s, sought to improve the local economy by establishing industries, including a brewery, so he is shown holding... a mug of beer!

INSPIRING OFFSHOOTS

The *trompe-l'oeil* artists obviously enjoyed the juxtaposition between their very convincing imitations and the real structures and building materials located just nearby. Real paving stones, for example – on the ground in front of the wall – seem to continue into the painted road depicted in the mural (see the photo of kids playing hockey). In another part of the painting, the artists have depicted a three-dimensional street lamp that seems truly to project out toward us. On the other side of the mural, beside the portrait of Governor Frontenac, there is a real street lamp, made of metal and glass, which lights up at night!

Since the completion of this work of art, a number of other *trompe l'oeil* murals have been created in the city. Perhaps the most inspiring offshoot of *La Fresque des Québécois* project came about when two of the Quebec artists who had worked on this first *trompe-l'oeil* mural obtained a grant to train disadvantaged street kids to paint a series of extraordinary murals in the St. Roch District. They chose a most unlikely location to create these new works of art, bringing magic and beauty to what is usually one of the ugliest places in any city: the concrete pillars that support a highway overpass.

PLACE ROYALE

BIRTHPLACE OF NEW FRANCE

The market square in the lower town first acquired the name *Place Royale* (Royal Square) when a bust of Louis XIV was installed there in 1686. During the French regime this open space, surrounded by fine merchants' houses, was a centre of public life. A farmers' market was held there twice a week and it was at *Place Royale* that the government made its announcements. It was also there that public punishments and executions were carried out, to set an example. A farmers' market was also held in the square during the British regime, and with the expansion of the port the sector became a hive of commercial activity in the early 19th century. After the 1860s, however, the port began to decline, and by the 20th century, the population had dwindled considerably and the area had become run down.

Then, during the 1960s and 70s, the government of Quebec undertook a major project: to attempt to restore to *Place Royale* the appearance it might have had during the French period. With great expense and effort, this dilapidated part of town was transformed into a potent symbol of French heritage. To local citizens and visitors alike, probably no place evokes the atmosphere of 17th and 18th century New France more than this picturesque square in the lower town. And yet, beneath the surface, the identity of this "cradle of French civilization in North America" is more complex than it might first appear. The present appearance of *Place Royale* can tell us as much about modern Quebec society – and our changing attitudes towards history and architectural preservation – as it can about the urban environment of the French regime.

ROYAL SQUARE OR MARKET SQUARE?

This square was not always called *Place Royale*. In fact, for most of its history it was known by more modest names, such as *Place du Marché*, (Market Square) and *Place de la Basse-Ville* (Lower Town Square). Even during the brief time from 1686 to about 1700, when the original bust of the king graced the square, few people referred to the site as *Place Royale*. After the bust was removed, the square's royal associations were quickly forgotten. It was not until 1937, six years after the bronze copy of Bernini's portrait of the king was installed, that the site was officially re-baptized *Place Royale*.

THE BUST OF LOUIS XIV

In 1685, Louis XIV's minister, the Marquis de Louvois, ordered that statues of the Sun King be erected in public squares throughout the realm. Over the next two years, then, stone and bronze portraits of the monarch were erected in such cities as Le Havre, Lyon – even far away Quebec, the capital of New France – so that all French citizens, no matter how far they lived from the splendour of Versailles, would recognize the image of their sovereign.

In 1686, Jean Bochart de Champigny, Intendant of New France, installed a bust of Louis XIV in the market square of Quebec's lower town. But the monument did not remain there for long. Merchants complained that it took up too much space on market days so it was

removed to the Intendant's Palace, around the year 1700. The bronze portrait may have been lost in a fire that destroyed the palace in 1713.

The present bust of Louis XIV in Quebec's Place Royale is a remarkable work of art. In the 1660s, the great Italian baroque sculptor Lorenzo Bernini went to Paris to participate in an architectural competition for an enlargement of the Louvre. Bernini's design was not chosen, but he did have time to carve a superb marble bust of the king which can be seen in Versailles today. Over the years, a number of fine bronze copies were made. One of them is now on display at the National Gallery, in Washington, D.C., while the bust in Quebec City's Place Royale was given to the Province of Quebec by the government of France in 1928.

Architecture for New France

Many of the first houses constructed around the square in the early 17th century were built with half-timber construction. Walls constructed by this method were made with wooden frames composed of a series of upright posts, with the spaces between them filled with stone and mortar. This ancient building technique had evolved in France over the centuries to compensate for a lack of wood, as the country's forests became depleted. Half-timber construction is typical of the traditional architecture of Normandy, where many examples of this age-old method of construction can still be seen today.

But half-timber construction turned out to be less appropriate for New France, where contrasts between cold and hot weather were much greater than in the mother country. Here, extreme changes in temperature caused construction materials to expand and contract considerably, so that gaps quickly developed between the wood frame and stone-and-mortar fill, letting in the cold winter air. With time, as builders learned to adapt to local conditions, they turned away from this traditional method and began to construct their buildings entirely in wood. With an almost unlimited supply available from the abundant forests of New France, it made little sense to continue with half-timber construction. Nevertheless, when fire became a serious cause for concern, more and more people started to build their houses in stone.

SNOW AND FIRE

As in northern France, Quebec houses were constructed with steep roofs, so that the snow would slide off easily. The photograph above illustrates

four roofing materials that were used during the French regime - from left to right: wooden planks, slate tiles, metal sheeting and wooden shingles. Ladders, attached to the steep roofs by metal hooks, provided easier access to do maintenance work, clean chimneys, or fight fires. Notice, also, the stone firewalls rising above the roof level. In cities of the past, with their narrow streets and densely packed buildings, fire was a constant threat. With stables filled with hay, fireplaces used for cooking and candles used to provide light, fires could easily break out. The danger was even greater in a northern city like Quebec, where it was necessary to keep fires going throughout much of the year to provide heat. The authorities of New France introduced legislation to diminish the risk of fires. They restricted the use of inflam-mable materials and required that stone firewalls be constructed to help stop flames from spreading from one house to another.

In 1682, a great fire swept through the lower town, destroying over 50 houses. One of the main reasons why this blaze turned into a disastrous confla-gration was that wooden shingles, being very light, were carried skyward by the hot air, spreading flames everywhere. After this terrible fire, wooden shingles were forbidden. Many people continued to use them, though, because they were relatively inexpensive. The legislation banning shingles must have been hard to enforce, because it had to be re-introduced a number of times.

A BUILDING CODE FOR NEW FRANCE

In 1727, after another huge fire in Montreal, Intendant Claude Dupuy enacted a more extensive building code, forbidding the construction of wooden frames around doors and windows, and of all external ornamentation made of wood. The building regulations also required that the floors of attics be lined with a thick layer of fireproof mortar. It was hoped that this would protect the rest of the building from spreading flames, even if the roof began to burn. The use of wooden shingles (*facing page*) was strictly forbidden, once again...

Unfortunately, alternative fireproof materials were not available to most people at the time. Slate tiles were very expensive because they had

to be imported from France, and metal was not yet widely used as a roofing material in the colony. The authorities decided to tolerate the use of wooden planks, until a better solution could be found. Why would planks be any better than wooden shingles?

PRIMITIVE FIRE FIGHTING TECHNIQUES

Wooden planks were thicker, so they might not catch fire as easily. They were also heavier, so they were less likely to be carried upward by the heat of a fire, and spread the flames. Most important, however, wooden planks were easier to tear down in an emergency. Dupuy's rules called for roof structures to be simplified, so that they

could be demolished quickly. Mansard roofs, which required heavy, complex wooden structures, were henceforth forbidden.

When a fire broke out, it was everyone's duty to rush to the scene with buckets of water, to try to douse the flames. Carpenters and builders were expected to bring their axes, hooks and lines to help pull down burning planks and roof structures. With no running water, and such primitive fire fighting techniques, there was probably little hope of saving a burning house. It was crucial, however, to try to stop the flames from spreading. If there was strong wind, hundreds of houses could easily be lost in a single fire.

With time, metal sheeting became the most popular material for roofing. Metal was light, durable and fireproof. General use of metal sheeting only became possible after 1742, when the French military engineer Gaspard Chaussegros de Léry developed a roofing technique adapted to Quebec's severe climate. After observing that soldered joints tended to break when exposed to extreme changes in temperature, he invented a method of attaching the sheets based on a folding technique. Despite technological improvements since that time, variations of this roofing method are still in use today. A good roofer always considers the direction of the prevailing winds when he decides how to position the overlapping sheets of metal. This roofing technique is called *tôle à la canadienne*, or "metal roofing Canadian style."

CREATING AN IMAGE OF NEW FRANCE

This watercolour (*facing page, bottom right*) painted by British officer James Pattison Cockburn around 1830, shows the market square when the steeple of *Notre-Dame-des-Victoires* church was still the tallest structure in the lower town. Historic images of *Place Royale* show that originally all the houses around the square were covered with a protective coating of white mortar, called *crépi*. In the 1960s, however, those responsible for restoring these buildings chose to remove this traditional material to reveal the stone walls underneath, which people at that time found attractive. The decision to uncover the rough stone had more to do with late 20th-century tastes than with the real history of the houses around the square.

In a more recent restoration (*facing page, above*), the whitewashed mortar was retained. Notice how the dressed stone around the window and along the corner of the building is set off nicely by the contrasting white *crépi*. Dressed stone ornamentation at the corners of buildings, laid so that the faces of the stones are alternatively large and small, is referred to by the architectural term "quoins", derived from the French word *coin*, or corner.

In Cockburn's watercolour of the square, the building in the left foreground displays quoins, providing an attractive contrast to the whitewashed mortar masonry. Notice also how the gray stone trim of *Notre-Dame-des-Victoires* church stands out against the white *crépi*. Cockburn's animated view shows the square on a Sunday, when so many people have come to pray in the little church that many are obliged to remain outside and kneel on the pavement.

A CHANGING URBAN ENVIRONMENT

Because Dupuy's building codes were so well-adapted to the specific conditions of this northern colonial city, they continued to influence building practices here long after the fall of New France. However, by the second half of the 19th century, the character of Quebec's lower town began to change considerably with the introduction of new building types of a very different shape and scale which towered over the older buildings in the sector. Large warehouses and offices were constructed, and many existing buildings were altered, as steep gable roofs were removed to make way for additional floors crowned by flat roofs and massive horizontal cornices.

In the 20th century the pace of change accelerated. Many historic houses were demolished and parts of the city underwent radical transformation, with the construction of tall buildings and highways. It was in this context of rapid modernization, which led to a growing concern about the future of the city's architectural heritage, that the historic district of Old Quebec was created in 1963. Soon afterwards, a major project was undertaken to recreate an image of New France at *Place Royale*.

The provincial government purchased over 60 buildings with the intention of restoring to the sector the appearance it might have had during the French Regime. Too often, in the early stages of the project, this meant destroying evidence of the real history of the site to create an image of an idealized, more distant past. Nineteenth-century buildings and ornamentation, considered to be without historic or architectural value, were demolished, and replaced by reconstructions of 18th century houses. While this approach enjoyed public support in its first phases, the extreme cost of the project, and the massive demolitions that it entailed, became a subject of considerable controversy by the end of the 1970s.

CHANGING APPROACHES TO RESTORATION

Architectural historians began to ask whether there was danger of creating a kind of "Disneyland" at *Place Royale*, where no one would know what was old and what was new. Finally, in 1978, a conference was held to determine the future of the site. The general consensus at the end of this meeting was that restoration efforts should show respect for the architecture of all of Quebec's history, not just that of the French Regime.

RENEWED RESPECT FOR 19TH-CENTURY ARCHITECTURE

The five-storey *Crédit Foncier* building (*below, left*), constructed in 1872, was purchased by the government of Quebec in the 1960s so that it could be demolished and replaced by a reconstruction of an 18th-century house. Large-scale demolitions, however, had fallen out of favour since the 1978 conference, and the edifice was allowed to remain standing. With time, the building, which had been constructed according the plans of architect Joseph-Ferdinand Peachy, came to be seen as a fine example of 19th-century architecture. In 2008, it was transformed into an apartment building, with shops on the ground floor. Now called the *Maison Paré*, the project was recognized by the City of Quebec in 2009, as a model of respectful restoration.

BUILDINGS EVOLVE OVER TIME

If we compare restoration efforts during the first phase of the *Place Royale* project, in the 1960s and 70s, with those done after the 1978 conference, we find that the treatment of certain architectural features differs considerably. For example, this window (*below, far right*) with its small panes of glass, typical of the 18th century, is located on the ground floor of the *Maison Fornel*, reconstructed in the early 1960s. On the other hand, more recent restorations have retained commercial shop windows typical of the 19th century. When large sheets of plate glass became available at a reasonable cost, in the 1840s, many shop owners chose to modify the ground floors of their buildings so that they could sell their goods more easily. When the *Maison Smith* (*below, left and facing page*) was restored in 1996, its 19th-century commercial façade, with large plate-glass windows and elaborate wooden ornamentation, was retained. This more recent restoration project, which retains elements from different periods of the history of the *Maison Smith*, acknowledges that buildings do not "freeze" at a specific moment in time. They evolve over the years, with changes in technology and lifestyle.

THE LOUIS XIV HOTEL

The Louis XIV Hotel (*left*) was a five-storey building that stood at the corner of *rue Notre-Dame* and *Place Royale*, until it was destroyed by fire in 1966. The edifice had actually begun as two houses, dating from the late 17th and early 18th centuries. They had been combined and enlarged over the years, then covered with a layer of mortar to disguise the changes that had been made. After a fire gutted the building, the government of Quebec decided to "restore" the site to the appearance that it would have had during the French regime. Today, the *Maison Dumont* (*below, left*) and the *Maison Picard*, beside it, occupy the site. While the *Maison Dumont* still retains certain elements of the original building, the *Maison Picard* is a complete reconstruction.

NEW USES FOR 19ᵀᴴ-CENTURY BUILDINGS

The massive restoration/reconstruction project that began at *Place Royale* in the 1960s caused considerable social disruption. Efforts were made to invite residents to return to their former homes after the work was completed, but there is no doubt that the project exacerbated a decline of the population that had already been underway for some years.

Fortunately, this trend began to reverse in the 1980s. At that time, as a renewed respect for 19th century architecture began to take hold, the abandoned warehouses in the sector, with their large windows and high ceilings, began to be seen with new eyes. Instead of being demolished, as had been originally planned, they were transformed into condominiums and cooperative housing projects, and played a key role in efforts to renew the population of the lower town.

In this view of the *Place Royale* sector, seen from the *Parc Montmorency* (*above*), the houses in the foreground are typical of the domestic-scale buildings that dominated Quebec's lower town during the French regime, while the larger block-shaped buildings are typical of the 19th century. In the background, a large cruise ship makes use of the deepwater docking facilities installed in the Old Port in 1984, when Quebec City celebrated the 450th anniversary of French explorer Jacques Cartier's first voyage to Canada. The new quays included beautiful pedestrian promenades that have made the waterfront accessible to local citizens and visitors alike.

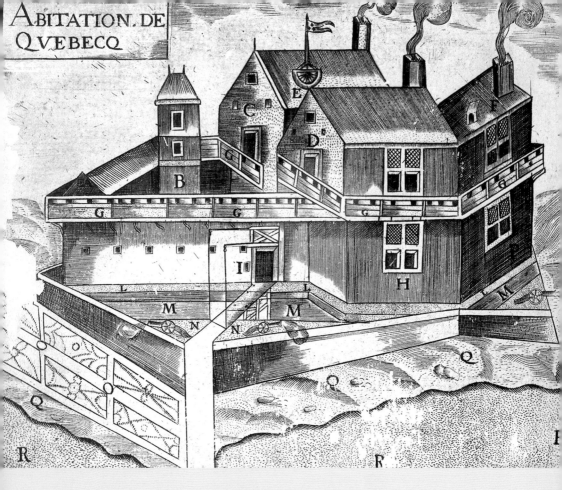

Beneath Place Royale

Archaeological remains found at *Place Royale* indicate that native peoples visited the site at least 3000 years ago, long before the arrival of the Europeans. Archaeologists have found tools made of stone and bone, clay pipes and other objects. They have also discovered the remains of a native burial site dating back approximately 1000 years.

CHAMPLAIN'S *HABITATION*

A woodcut (*above*) from a book published by Samuel de Champlain in 1613 shows his first *Habitation*, which served as a warehouse, fortress and place of residence for his men. It was constructed of wood, and did not stand up very

well to the rain and snow of Quebec. When the wood began to rot, he replaced this first building, in 1624, with a stronger structure made of stone, with round towers for defence.

Inscribed in the pavement of the square, in front of *Notre-Dame-des-Victoires* church, is a circle in dark stone (*facing page top*) which marks the place where, in 1976, archaeologists excavated one of the towers of Champlain's second building. The remains of the tower are still located below the pavement. A photograph, taken during the dig (*facing page, centre*), shows the tower as the archaeologists found it. Among objects found on the site was a 17th -century rosary cross, shown here in a drawing (*facing page, far right*).

Observe how the dark lines in the pavement (*left, top*) indicate how the stone foundation walls of Champlain's *Habitation* continue under the wall of *Notre-Dame-des-Victoires* church. In 1682, the *Habitation* (which, by that time, had been transformed into the King's Storehouse) was badly damaged by a major fire in the lower town. After the fire, the building was taken down, but parts of the foundation walls were kept, to support the new church that was built to replace it.

VAULTED BASEMENTS

In order to help prevent the spread of fires, building codes in New France (*see pages 54-55*) required that houses be built of stone, on high, vaulted basements. In addition to being fireproof, these cellars (*bottom*), with their curved stone ceilings, protected the buildings from dampness and – unlike ceilings supported by wooden beams – they were not subject to rot.

Vaulted basements, extremely solid, could support huge weights and provide shelter from bombardments in times of war. These cellars maintained a steady, cool temperature of approximately 14-15 degrees centigrade throughout the year, making them a good location to store wine and other provisions.

Notre-Dame-des-Victoires

WORSHIP AND CONFLICT

Originally *l'Église de l'Enfant Jésus*, (The Church of the Christ Child), the name of this church was changed twice, after two victories over the English: first, to *Notre-Dame-de-la-Victoire*, (Our Lady of Victory) and then to *Notre-Dame-des-Victoires*, (Our Lady of Victories). For most of the 17th century there had been no church to serve the lower town. Worshippers were obliged to walk up the steep *Côte de la Montagne* to reach Notre-Dame-de-Québec – a difficult climb, especially for children and the elderly during the icy winter months. So, in 1680, Bishop Laval wrote to the king requesting permission to build a church in the lower town. Space became available two years later, after a huge fire swept through the sector, but it was not until 1688 that construction of the new church finally began.

The bell tower and steeple (*facing page*) were constructed between 1858 and 1861, following the plans of architect Joseph Ferdinand Peachy. A wrought-iron cross (*left*), adorned with the fleur-de-lis – a centuries-old symbol of France – supports a weather vane in the form of a golden cock. The cock reminds worshippers of the words spoken by Jesus to Peter during the Last Supper: "Before a cock crows, you will deny me three times." Matthew 26:34

A MODEST EXTERIOR

The original plans for the church, prepared by architect Claude Baillif in 1687, had called for an elegant classical façade, in finely-cut stone. But resources were limited at that time, and not until 1723 was the church finally completed in a simplified form. Constructed by architect Jean Maillou, it was built with rough stone walls, covered with a layer of whitewashed mortar. Ornamentation was reduced to three niches for statues, with a bull's-eye window over the entrance portal.

DESTRUCTION BY FIRE BOMBS AND CHANGES OVER THE YEARS

An engraving (above), made after a detailed drawing by British naval officer Richard Short, shows the ruins of Notre-Dame-des-Victoires after the bombardment of 1759. English firebombs have destroyed the church and the houses surrounding Place Royale, leaving only the stone walls still standing.

In a recent photograph taken on a winter evening (facing page) lighting provided by the Commission de la capitale nationale du Québec highlights the bell tower and steeple that were added to the church in the mid-nineteenth century. A subtle line of white light, projected onto the ground in front of the church, marks the location where archaeologists found the remains of Champlain's second Habitation.

INTERIOR ORNAMENTATION

Architectural historian Jack Richardson once described Notre-Dame-des-Victoires church as a bit like grandfather's axe: the blade has been replaced many times, and the handle has been replaced many times... but it's still grandfather's axe. Although the church was first constructed in the late 17th century, most of the ornamentation of the interior (following pages) was sculpted by Raphaël Giroux, a disciple of architect Thomas Baillairgé, between 1854 and 1857.

THE TABERNACLE

The tabernacle, designed and sculpted by architect David Ouellet in 1878, is in the form of a medieval fortress supporting a statue of the Virgin Mary. She is flanked by golden angels holding flags indicating the dates of the two victories over the English: 1690 and 1711. Above the two angels, paintings of allegorical figures illustrate these French triumphs.

In the painting on the right-hand side, a woman wearing a crown bears a shield adorned with three fleurs-de-lis, celebrating the French victory of 1690, when an English fleet sailed up the St. Lawrence from Boston to attack Quebec but failed to take the city. Inspired by a medal struck by order of Louis XIV to commemorate the defeat of the English, the painting includes a text in Latin that reads: KEBEKA LIBERATA – "Quebec Liberated".

The painting on the left-hand side refers to a second English attempt on the city, in 1711. Another fleet of warships left Boston to attack Quebec, but never got there. The invading force became lost in a thick fog on the St. Lawrence and a number of the ships ran aground and sank. Over a thousand men drowned, and what remained of the English fleet turned around and went back to Boston.

No matter whether you are French, British, American or Russian, there is always a tendency to believe that God is on your side in time of war. The French were convinced that they had been saved by divine intervention, so the painting depicts a warrior angel, sending an English ship to the bottom of the St. Lawrence.

EX VOTOS

Suspended from the ceiling of the church is a large model of the Brézé (*facing page and detail above*), a 17th-century French warship. This is an ex voto – a gift given to the church in thanks for a favour obtained. In 1664, the Marquis de Tracy, a viceroy, was sent to Quebec City to take charge of the French troops in North America. After a difficult journey, he gave thanks to God for his safe arrival by having a model of the ship constructed, and suspending it from the ceiling of the cathedral in the upper town. It remained there until 1759, when English fire-bombs came crashing through the roof. The ship fell to the floor, shattering into pieces. The broken model was taken to the Seminary, next door, where it remained until the 1950s, when it was finally restored and suspended from the ceiling of *Notre-Dame-des-Victoires*. It is

one of the most fascinating objects to have survived in Quebec City from the 17th century.

Other ex votos can be seen in *Notre-Dame des Victoires* church. A painting depicts a ship in distress on a stormy sea. Written in the left hand corner are the words EX VOTO. Dated 1747, the text tells us that this simple work of art was made at the request of Captain Simonin, in thanks for having survived a terrible storm. In the sky above can be seen the Virgin Mary, holding the Christ Child, intervening to save the endangered vessel. Ex votos in the form of stone plaques on the walls of the church (*below*) express the thanks of worshippers who were cured of various illnesses.

PLACE DE PARIS

A DIALOGUE WITH HISTORY

The *Place de Paris*, or "Paris Square", in Quebec's lower town, was inaugurated in 1987 by Jacques Chirac, Mayor of Paris and Prime Minister of France. A symbol of friendship between two French-speaking cities, the new square was intended to complement *Place du Québec*, which had been established four years earlier in the Saint-Germain-des-Prés district of Paris. The central element of Quebec's *Place de Paris* is a gift from the City of Paris: a contemporary sculpture by French artist Jean-Pierre Raynaud, entitled "A Dialogue with History". Erected in honour of the first French explorers, this abstract work of art, clad in white marble and black granite, stands in striking contrast to its historic surroundings. It is as though the creator of this 20th-century sculpture has sought to enter into a dialogue with the 17th century, personified by the bust of Louis XIV in nearby *Place Royale*.

RECLAIMED FROM THE RIVER

If you had wanted to stand here in the early 19th century, you would have had to tread water! Compare a contemporary photograph of this site (*facing page, bottom left*) with an 1829 watercolour by James Pattison Cockburn (*facing page, top*). His painting depicts a sandy beach just in front of the same stone houses that border the square today. At high tide, in Cockburn's time, the location of today's *Place de Paris* was completely covered by the waters of the St. Lawrence. In the foreground of the painting is a ferryboat that was driven, literally, by "horse power". Horses walked in a circle, activating a mechanism that powered the blades of a paddlewheel. While it seems hard to believe today, the slow-moving "horse boat" was able to cross the St. Lawrence River, providing a ferry service used mainly by farmers to transport livestock and produce. Just in front of the houses is a small market building with stairs leading down to the shore below. The staircase allowed farmers to unload produce directly from their boats – whether the tide was high or low.

The bay depicted in Cockburn's watercolour was filled in during the 1840s, and a larger market building was constructed on the site in 1850-51. An image of the new Finlay Market (*above*) shows another broad flight of steps leading into the water. Those stairs were located at the edge of the present site of *Place de Paris*, where cars now drive by on Dalhousie Street, a busy thoroughfare located on land reclaimed from the St. Lawrence River. The building was demolished in 1906 but the location continued to serve as an outdoor fruit and vegetable market for many years afterward. The site was later used as a parking lot before finally being transformed into *Place de Paris* in 1987. A photograph (*facing page, bottom right*) shows how, in the past, stone masons often rounded off the lower corners of houses to enable wagons to pass more easily.

Batterie
Royale

DEFENDING THE LOWER TOWN

The *Batterie Royale* (Royal Gun Battery) was built in 1691 to bolster the defences of the lower town after a British attack in 1690. Constructed on a rocky point, this fortification was originally surrounded by water on all sides but one. Exposed to wind and waves throughout the year, the *Batterie Royale* was particularly vulnerable during the winter months, when portions of the masonry were often carried away by the ice. Expensive and difficult to maintain, the battery was constantly in need of repair, which caused headaches for generations of French military engineers. The *Batterie Royale* saw heavy action during the siege of 1759, but when the fighting was over, the British authorities seem to have decided that its location was more important for trade than for defence.

By 1763, they had already allowed warehouses to be constructed on the battery, and in 1785, part of the structure disappeared from view when a dock was built in front of it. By the 1840s, the old French fortification had been completely covered over.

Archaeologists uncovered the remains of the *Batterie Royale* in the 1970s and it was reconstructed on its original foundations in 1977. The battery is now armed with reproductions of French cannons, gifts to Quebec from the government of France.

The present restoration shows us how the fortification might have looked during peacetime. When an attack was expected, certain modifications had to be made. To strengthen the structure against enemy fire, earth had to be piled up behind the stone merlons (the walls that separate the open-

ings for the cannons). Wickerwork baskets filled with earth, called gabions, had to be placed beside the cannons, to protect the gun crews. Gabions served the same purpose as do today's sandbags in modern warfare. Note that the sides of the embrasures (openings for the cannons) are lined with brick, which was considered less dangerous than stone when struck by enemy fire.

Centuries of landfill operations have left the *Batterie Royale* far from the shoreline but you can still get a sense of how the fortification would have looked when it was surrounded by the waters of the St. Lawrence (*above*). The ditch beside the battery fills up each day at high tide, when water infiltrates beneath the modern docks and the road, reaching the walls of the fortification, as it did during the French regime.

MAISON CHEVALIER

INTERIORS FROM THE PAST

In 1752, Jean-Baptiste Chevalier, merchant, built a large stone house at the water's edge, facing *Cul-de-Sac* bay, one of the busiest "ports" in Quebec's lower town. The *Maison Chevalier* has survived to this day, but the building and its surroundings have changed considerably since the 18th century. The bay was filled in during the 1850s to allow a large market building to be constructed on the site (*see page 92*), leaving the 18th-century residence far from the new shoreline. As today's pedestrians stroll along the curved sidewalk in front of the *Maison Chevalier*, they are following the original profile of the vanished beach of *Cul de Sac* bay.

In 1806, the French-regime residence was converted into the London Coffee House, a celebrated inn and tavern which appears in a number of 19th-century images of the lower town. In those days, the site of today's *Maison Chevalier* was occupied by three houses whose principal entrance doors faced a narrow lane called the *Rue Cul-de-Sac*, depicted in a 1929 drawing by Barbara H. Stephens and a contemporary photograph (*pages 90-91*).

The *Maison Chevalier* acquired its present appearance in 1959, when the original three houses were combined to form a single edifice, in an effort to create the appearance of an elegant 18th-century aristocratic residence, or *hôtel particulier*. The residence constructed in 1752 by Jean-Baptiste Chevalier now forms the left-hand side of the building, while the right-hand side is composed of the former *Maison Frérot*, built in the 1680's, and the *Maison Chesnay*, a reconstruction of a 17th-century house. Admittedly, by today's standards, the true history of the site was distorted to a certain extent by this 1959 "restoration". Nevertheless, the project was the first to acknowledge the importance of Quebec's surviving French heritage, and represented the first step towards the revitalization of the lower town.

PLEASE COME IN...

Period rooms in the *Maison Chevalier*, now integrated into the *Musée de la Civilisation*, contain furniture and objects that evoke changing fashions and social customs in Quebec City during the French and British regimes. The display on the ground floor represents the interior of

the 18th-century residence of a well-to-do French merchant. On the second floor, we enter a modest 19th-century interior with furniture made of pine and other Canadian wood. Finally, visitors can view an upper-class British interior, with elegant furniture made with exotic imported woods.

The Home of an 18th-century French Merchant

During the French Regime it was common practice to place the owner's bed in the same room where guests were received and dinner was served (*facing page*). The green curtains surrounding this impressive four-poster bed would have been of crucial importance during Quebec's severe winters. Seeking protection from the extreme cold, some people even slept in a "cabin bed": a wooden box, similar in size to a four-poster bed, but provided with hinged doors. Enclosed beds also provided a minimum of intimacy in such multi-functional rooms. House owners in the 18th century often lived in close proximity with tenants, servants and apprentices. It seems they were not nearly as concerned with privacy as we are today.

The two-tiered buffet in the background dates from the late 17th century. This type of buffet was used to store linen and dishes. The table in the centre of the room (*right top*) is set for a meal, with pewter dishes and cutlery. The chairs, which are made of Canadian pine, show a Louis XIII influence, with turned legs and an H-shaped understructure, to provide extra strength and solidity. In the background, a low buffet, decorated with a diamond-point motif, is also of Louis XIII inspiration.

Kitchen utensils (*right, centre*), are hung by the kitchen fireplace. The *crémaillère* (*right, bottom*), was used to used to hang cooking pots over the flames. Today the expression "*pendre la crémaillère*" (to hang up the *crémaillère*, or trammel) is still used in French-speaking countries to describe a house-warming party.

A Modest 19th-Century Interior

The furniture and objects displayed here evoke the atmosphere of a modest 19th-century common room, in which local French traditions are combined with new influences from the British Isles and the United States. The design of the rocking chair (*facing page, middle right*) near the window is based on an American model, known as a Windsor "comb-back" because the spindles that form the back of the chair resemble a comb.

A makeshift ironing board (*facing page, bottom left*) composed of a plank placed on two chairs, stands in front of a two-tiered cast iron stove made in Quebec City around 1840. This type of stove was so efficient that, even on the coldest winter days, visitors from Europe often complained about the stifling heat. Cast-iron stoves also provided a convenient place to heat irons (*facing page, bottom right*).

A genre scene (*above*), by Cornelius Krieghoff, gives us a sense of how people would have lived in the kind of 19th-century interior evoked in this period room.

An Upper-Class British Interior

British aristocrats came to Quebec in the service of their country, as military officers and colonial administrators, while others, from humbler backgrounds, came here hoping to make their fortunes in the fur trade, timber trade, or shipbuilding. Members of the colonial elite, and those who aspired to be so, provided their residences with elegant furniture made from mahogany and other exotic woods, just as their counterparts would have done at home in Great Britain.

In contrast to the multifunctional rooms and furniture that were typical of 18th-century Quebec residences, the rooms in fashionable 19th-century homes (dining room, library and others) were designed for specific activities. An array of specialized furniture was created for these rooms, such as the game table (*facing page, right centre*) in the foreground, with its green baize surface, suitable for playing cards. Notice also the elegant couch in

the foreground, a detail of which is shown (*facing page, bottom right*).

The Regency chairs in this early 19th-century interior have curved "sabre" legs inspired by classical models from ancient Greece. These are examples of the famous Trafalgar Chair, very popular in England during the first decades of the 19th century. The Trafalgar Chair is recognizable by its sculpted-rope motif (*facing page, bottom left*), which celebrates Admiral Nelson's victory over the French navy in the Battle of Trafalgar, in 1805.

The 1809 portrait of the Woolsey family (*above*), by William Berczy, shows the refined interior of an upper-class residence in Quebec City in the early 19th-century. The clothing and furniture reflect the cultivated environment of the Regency period in England, evoked in the novels of Jane Austen, and remembered today as the "Age of Elegance".

PETIT CHAMPLAIN QUARTER

COMMERCE AND CRAFTSMEN

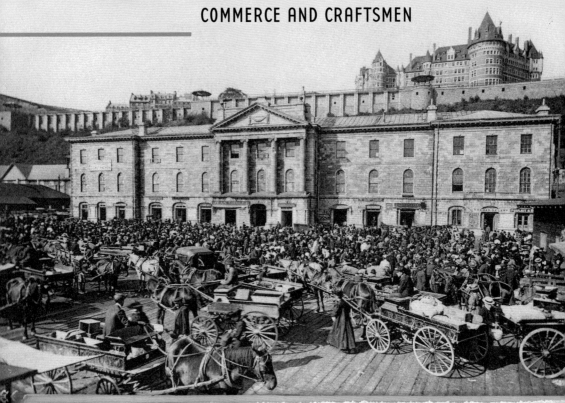

For centuries this waterfront district bustled with the activities of sailors, craftsmen and merchants, all of whose livelihood depended on navigation and the maritime trade. Here, warships were constructed for the king of France in the 18th century; in the 19th century ship chandlers provided supplies for square-riggers bound for Great Britain; and here, generations of farmers from the surrounding region arrived by boat to sell their produce (*above*). Toward the end of the 19th century the neighbourhood began to fall on hard times, but today, with its craftsmen's workshops, boutiques, bistros and restaurants, the *Petit Champlain* quarter is once again one of the most colourful and animated corners of the Old City.

In the early 17th century there was a simple pathway here, leading along the shore from Champlain's *Habitation* (*see pages 62-63*) to a spring at the base of the cliff, known as "Champlain's Fountain". The street that developed on the site of that path came to be known as *Rue Champlain*. In 1688, it was re-named *Rue de Meulles*, in memory of the king's administrator, Jacques de Meulles, who had served as Intendant of New France from 1682 to 1686. Nevertheless, many people continued to call the street by its original name. By the end of the 18th century it was once again officially called *Rue Champlain*.

As in nearby *Place Royale*, most of the first houses along the street were built with the half-timber technique, or entirely of wood. However, after the great fire of 1682, regulations required that buildings be constructed with fireproof materials, so that by the middle of the 18th century, many of the houses had been rebuilt in stone. Nevertheless, the southern extremity of the street remained

filled with small wooden houses and tumbledown shacks, occupied by some of the city's poorest residents. In 1747, some houses were demolished when part of the area was taken over to establish a royal shipyard. Despite these changes the sector remained one of the most densely populated neighbourhoods in the city during the last decades of the French Regime.

Rapid expansion of the port under the British led to an even greater concentration of mariners and craftsmen. Many Irish immigrants found work on the docks and settled their families in this modest neighbourhood, seen in this early 20th-century photograph (*facing page, top*) when the street was paved with wooden planks.

In the 1850s, *Cul de Sac* bay was filled in to allow construction of an impressive market building for the burgeoning population of the lower town. Constructed between 1858 and 1860, the new *Marché Champlain* (*see page 92*), with its fine cut-stone façade, portico and triangular pediment, was designed to present a dignified image for visitors arriving in Quebec City via the port. Despite its grandeur, however, during the 19th century this imposing edifice was often humorously described by locals as the city's least expensive building. The fine stone, great columns and other architectural elements had all been recuperated from the charred ruins of the Parliament building, which had been destroyed by a fire in 1854, for only $100!

To provide better access to the new *Marché Champlain*, a wide street was opened along the waterfront. The civic authorities decided to call this new thoroughfare *Rue Champlain*, and to re-name the narrow, older street at the base of the cliff *Rue Petit-Champlain*, or "Little Champlain Street".

REBIRTH OF A NEIGHBOURHOOD

The market building was torn down in 1910 and plans to build a large railway terminus here in the early 20th century almost led to the demolition of the entire sector. Although the area was saved from destruction, it nevertheless experienced a period of severe decline in the decades that followed. By the 1960s and 1970s many of the buildings in the neighbourhood were empty and abandoned.

In the mid-1970s, two visionaries – architect Jacques de Blois and local businessman Gerry Paris – began to purchase some of the dilapidated properties in the sector. Inspired by revitalization efforts they had seen in other port cities, the private developers proposed a project that stood in striking contrast to the massive government project underway at nearby *Place Royale*. Rather than demolish 19th-century buildings to create an image of New France, as the government was doing, de Blois and Paris decided simply to repair existing structures as they found them – at a much more reasonable cost – then invite artisans to set up their apartments, workshops and boutiques in the restored buildings. The project involved considerable risk for its developers, but de Blois and Paris succeeded in bringing new life to this rundown sector, while at the same time, preserving its authentic 18th, 19th and 20th century architecture, in all its diversity. In 1985, the resident artisans and small business owners formed a cooperative and purchased the restored buildings from the developers. Today this once-dilapidated sector, now a thriving commercial and residential neighbourhood, is seen as a model of sensitive and respectful urban revitalization.

RUE SAINT-PIERRE

THE WALL STREET OF QUEBEC

D uring the French Regime, *Rue St-Pierre* (St. Peter Street) was home to some of Quebec's most prominent citizens, including colonial administrators, military officers and prosperous merchants. At first the street could not be extended much further than the *Côte de la Montagne*. Beyond that point the waters of the St. Lawrence covered the shoreline twice a day, at high tide. By the early 18th century, however, landfill operations made it possible to push the street further north along the shoreline, as merchants built stone quays in front of their properties, so that boats could tie up at their private docks.

BANKING AND BUSINESS

The imposing columns and stone carvings that embellish the commercial buildings along *Rue St-Pierre* evoke the great days of the 19th-century port of Quebec, when the city's economy was based on the timber trade and shipbuilding. Although activity in the port declined after the 1860s, *Rue St-Pierre* continued to serve as the city's main business street until well into the 20th century. So many banks, insurance companies and warehouses were built on this busy thoroughfare that it came to be known as "the Wall Street of Quebec".

In the second half of the 20th century, however, businesses began to move away from this sector of the Old City, and many fine buildings were left behind, empty and abandoned. Fortunately, beginning in the 1980s, the area experienced a renaissance and many historic buildings were converted to new uses. Today, architects' offices, condominiums, galleries, shops and boutique hotels have brought new life into the area, making *Rue St-Pierre* a fashionable address once more.

A Changing Streetscape

The size and scale of the houses located at the south end of *Rue St-Pierre* (*above*), give us a good idea of how the street might have looked during the 18th and early 19th centuries. The red-roofed stone buildings in the foreground were reconstructed in 1976 to evoke the appearance they might have had in the 18th century, when this was the property of the ambitious French merchant Charles Guillemin. In 1713, Guillemin purchased a warehouse which had originally been built for the Jesuits in 1683. He then constructed a three-storey addition to accommodate his residence, shop and warehouse. Notice a low, windowless structure, projecting from the end of the warehouse; this was designed to store salt, which was used to preserve fish for export.

A comparison of two views of *Rue St-Pierre* illustrates how the business district evolved during the 19th and 20th centuries. When James Pattison Cockburn painted this watercolour in 1829 (*left*), most of the buildings along the street were domestic in scale, like the merchants' houses in nearby *Place Royale*. The owners of these buildings still followed the age-old tradition of living in one's place of business – with a shop on the ground floor, storage in the basement, and residential quarters in the upper storeys.

By the time William Notman took this photograph (*facing page, top*) in the early 20th century, the street had changed considerably in appearance. Most of the domestic-scale buildings had been replaced by much larger structures: banks, office buildings and warehouses. The residential component had all but disappeared, and *Rue St-Pierre* had become almost exclusively devoted to business.

Banks

The Molson Bank, established on *Rue St-Pierre* in the early 19th century (right, top), closely resembled neighbouring houses in shape and scale. Its facade, however, was given greater dignity by the addition of classical ornamentation, carved in wood, to proclaim that here was a prestigious, solid enterprise where clients could deposit their money with confidence. Just down the street, the Bank of British North America, built in 1850 by architect John Wells, is also domestic in scale. This time, however, the architect, born and trained in England, chose to enhance the grandeur of his building by giving it an elegant facade in cut stone, graced by columns and classical ornamentation.

By the 1860s, some of the banks along *Rue St-Pierre* were very impressive indeed. The Quebec Bank (*see pages 98-99*), across the street from the Molson Bank, was built in 1863 according to the plans of British architect Edward Staveley. His rather grand building, which would not have looked out of place among the great financial institutions of London, takes its architectural inspiration from 16th-century Italian Renaissance palaces designed by the celebrated architect Andrea Palladio.

The Quebec Bank, which had been founded in 1818 by local English-speaking businessmen, became a very successful enterprise and gradually expanded its operations across the country, opening branches in Ontario and the western provinces. Then, in 1912, it moved its headquarters to Montreal, which by that time had become the financial centre of Canada. However, more difficult years were to follow. Seriously challenged by increasing competition, the Quebec Bank was finally absorbed by the Royal Bank of Canada in 1917. The former Quebec Bank building has now been integrated into the *Musée de la civilisation*, providing office space for the museum staff.

Facing the intersection of *Rue St-Pierre* and *Rue de la Barricade* is another imposing bank building – a former branch of the Bank of Montreal (*right*), constructed according to the plans of architects Cox and Amos in 1906 – with a very handsome row of ionic columns in finely-cut limestone. The building later served as a branch of the Toronto Dominion Bank, before being converted into offices for an architectural firm. The photograph on the facing page depicts the impressive curved portico of the former Canadian Imperial Bank of Commerce (*see also page 131*).

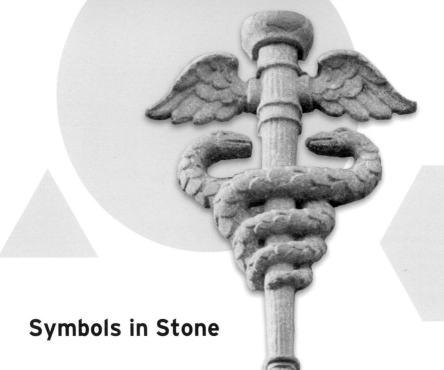

Symbols in Stone

In the 19th and early 20th centuries, it was common practice for business owners to advertise their commercial establishments with images of their impressive buildings. They hired prominent architects and invested large sums of money to construct these imposing edifices. Teams of talented sculptors and stonemasons were engaged to embellish the buildings with classical ornamentation and sculptures, designed to impress potential customers. Symbols, carved in stone, were intended to convey messages to pedestrians walking in the streets below.

The coat of arms of the Bank of Montreal (*below*) crowns the facade of another former bank building, constructed in 1927 according to the plans of architects Lawson and Little.

Flanked by two natives, an oval shield, supporting a Canadian beaver, displays the X-shaped cross of Saint Andrew, patron saint of Scotland. The shield is adorned with the emblems of four peoples: the Scottish thistle, the English rose, the Irish shamrock, and the French Fleur de Lys.

The symbol of commerce (*facing page, top*), which is often confused with a symbol of medicine, is carved in stone on the façades of a number of buildings in the old business district of the lower town. This example is displayed on the façade of the former Imperial Bank of Commerce, constructed in 1913. The symbol of commerce makes reference to the Greek God Hermes, known to the Romans as Mercury. Hermes, the messenger god, could fly through the skies, thanks to his winged helmet and winged sandals. The god of commerce and travel, he was also worshipped by thieves.

Lion's heads (above), carved in stone, flank the entrance of the former Bank of British North America, constructed in 1850. The lion, an emblem of Great Britain, was associated with royalty, power and courage.

Carved stone heads (*below*) look out from the façade of an 1863 warehouse/residence that is now part of the Auberge Saint-Antoine (*see pages 112-119*). The second head from the left represents the French explorer Jacques Cartier.

Tall Buildings

Designed by Joseph Ferdinand Peachy in 1866, the Union Bank Building (*left, top*), at the corner of *Rue Saint-Pierre* and *Côte de la Montagne*, originally had three floors, crowned by a mansard roof. After the invention of the elevator, this building was enlarged (*left, below*). The architect, Harry Staveley, added two floors, in 1897, replacing the mansard roof with a flat one adorned with an impressive cornice.

The *Caisse d'économie Notre-Dame-de-Quebec*, across the street, founded by French-speaking businessmen in 1848, was constructed according to the plans of Joseph Ferdinand Peachy in 1874. This building was enlarged in 1906 with the addition of a fifth storey designed by architect René P. Lemay. Faced with glazed terra cotta tiles, the top floor boasts an imposing bronze cornice (*facing page, centre right*), supported by a row of monumental consoles. This former bank has been converted into an apartment complex.

The Dominion Building (*facing page, left*), now an elegant boutique hotel (*Le Germain-Dominion*) was Quebec's first "skyscraper". Designed by architect René P. Lemay for the Dominion Fish & Fruit Company in 1912, this edifice is nine storeys high. Constructed with a modern steel frame, the building has an elaborate façade in glazed terra cotta (*detail, facing page, bottom right*). First used to adorn buildings thousands of years ago in ancient Egypt and Mesopotamia, terra cotta became very popular with early 20th-century architects, who considered it a "miracle" material. Manufactured using a moulding process, terra cotta tiles and decorative elements could be produced at a much lower cost than carved stone. Terra cotta was used to sheath the facades of famous skyscrapers, including the Woolworth Building in New York City, the tallest building in the world when it was erected in 1913 – one year after the construction of the Dominion Building on Quebec's *Rue St-Pierre*. Although terra cotta was well-suited to the hot dry climate of the Middle East, it did not stand up well to the rigours of North American winters. The façades of many early 20th-century buildings, such as this one, have thus deteriorated badly and have required extensive restoration work. Next door to the Dominion Building is the former Hochelaga Bank, which was constructed in 1901 (*top right*). This fine building, crowned by an impressive bronze railing, is now also part of the *Le Germain-Dominion*.

THE AMERICANS ATTACK

During the dark early-morning hours of the last day of the year 1775, in a blinding snowstorm, American revolutionaries launched an attack against the city of Quebec. This image depicts the revolutionaries, led by Benedict Arnold, scaling a barrier at the base of the cliff – with the British waiting for them below. The Americans were defeated and many were killed or captured. The remaining revolutionary forces laid siege to the city for the rest of the winter but had to withdraw in the spring when British reinforcements arrived. The battle of December 31, 1775 is commemorated by bronze plaques on a house at the corner of Rue St-Pierre and Rue de la Barricade (the former Molson Bank, facing page and page 103), where the Americans were stopped by British soldiers and the local Canadian militia.

WAREHOUSES

STONE PALACES BY THE WATERFRONT

D uring the second half of the 19th century, massive stone warehouses were constructed along Quebec's waterfront. As in many other port cities at the time, the design of these great block-shaped buildings was inspired by the imposing architecture of Italian Renaissance palaces.

The Renaud warehouse, built in 1875 (*below*), was designed by Joseph Ferdinand Peachy. This building was originally divided into four individual stores, separated by firewalls. Only three sections remain; one portion was lost in a blaze, but a firewall protected the rest from de-

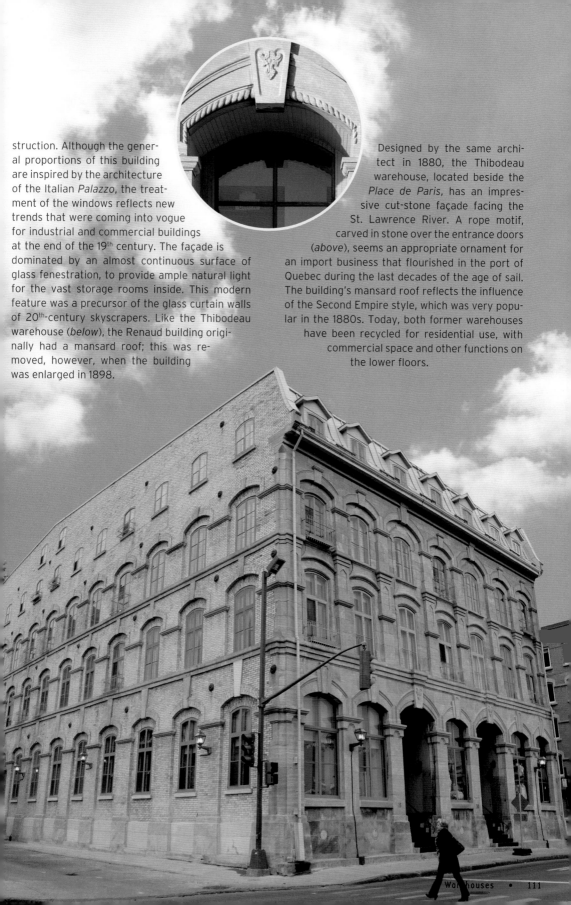

struction. Although the general proportions of this building are inspired by the architecture of the Italian *Palazzo*, the treatment of the windows reflects new trends that were coming into vogue for industrial and commercial buildings at the end of the 19th century. The façade is dominated by an almost continuous surface of glass fenestration, to provide ample natural light for the vast storage rooms inside. This modern feature was a precursor of the glass curtain walls of 20th-century skyscrapers. Like the Thibodeau warehouse (*below*), the Renaud building originally had a mansard roof; this was removed, however, when the building was enlarged in 1898.

Designed by the same architect in 1880, the Thibodeau warehouse, located beside the *Place de Paris*, has an impressive cut-stone façade facing the St. Lawrence River. A rope motif, carved in stone over the entrance doors (*above*), seems an appropriate ornament for an import business that flourished in the port of Quebec during the last decades of the age of sail. The building's mansard roof reflects the influence of the Second Empire style, which was very popular in the 1880s. Today, both former warehouses have been recycled for residential use, with commercial space and other functions on the lower floors.

AUBERGE
SAINT-ANTOINE
HERITAGE AND HOSPITALITY

T he *Auberge Saint-Antoine*, located in the heart of Quebec's historic waterfront sector, is both an elegant hotel and a fascinating museum that offers guests and visitors a unique opportunity to discover the history of the port of Quebec as it has evolved over more than three centuries. Hundreds of artefacts, found on the site by archaeologists, are displayed like works of art in museum-quality display cases – not only in public areas, such as the entrance lobby, but also in the hotel guest rooms. The creation of this unique hotel/museum, which combines contemporary architecture and design with an identity deeply rooted in the history of its site, was made possible through an inspired partnership between private enterprise and government.

The *Auberge* first opened its doors in 1992. At that time, the entrance lobby was located in the old Chillas warehouse, originally constructed for barrel-maker John Chillas in 1822. The former warehouse, the oldest of its kind remaining in the city, can be seen in the lower right-hand corner of this photograph. Today the Chillas building houses the hotel's celebrated *Panache* restaurant.

The first hotel rooms were established in a new red-brick building (to the left of the Chillas warehouse), facing the St. Lawrence River. In 1996 more rooms were added by integrating an historic house into the hotel complex. The house, constructed for the Hunt family in 1836, contains elements

of an older residence which was built in the 1720s. Located at the end of the property, on the corner of *Rue Saint-Antoine* and *Rue Saint-Pierre*, the Hunt house remained separated from the rest of the complex by a parking lot. Finally, in 2003, a new wing was constructed, linking the Hunt house, along with a former warehouse/residence built in 1863, (see page 119) with the initial phase of the *Auberge*. Today this unique museum/hotel, with its signature concept based on history and archaeology, has 95 rooms.

A STONE QUAY AND GUN BATTERY

A stone quay, constructed at the turn of the 18th-century and converted into a gun battery in 1709,

has been preserved, and integrated into the design of the hotel lobby (*above*). Over ten meters long, the remains of the *Batterie Dauphine* extend beyond the lobby into a sunken courtyard outside the hotel, facing *Rue Saint-Antoine*. The exterior portion is visible from the lobby through a glass curtain-wall. An additional stone wall can be seen in the exterior courtyard, running parallel to the street. This structure served as a buttress to support a second gun battery which was built in 1757. An 18th-century French cannon (*right*), found on the site, is displayed in the *Café Artefact* beside the remains of the quay and gun battery. A cannon ball, fired by the British against the lower town in 1759, is still attached to the splintered fragments of a wooden beam that it struck during the siege.

Artefacts (*clockwise from the right*): Corkscrew, date unknown; Bank token, worth a half penny, 1837; Dominoes, c.1825-1850; Candle snuffer; Padlock, wrought iron and brass, c. 1840; Wrought iron harpoon point c.1720-1725.

FIFTEEN YEARS OF ARCHAEOLOGICAL DIGS

During the early stages of the project, the Price family, owners of the *Auberge Saint-Antoine*, decided to allow archaeologists from the City of Quebec and Laval University to do extensive excavations on the site. Fourteen archaeological digs, carried out over a period of fifteen years, yielded a remarkable collection of artefacts spanning over three centuries. Rather than have these objects removed to a museum or storage facility, the Price family – in partnership with the city and the province of Quebec – conceived of a plan that would see the artefacts displayed on the very site where they had been found.

Display cases in the entrance lobby tell the story of the evolution of the port by means of three scale models that depict the site as it has changed over the centuries. The dioramas take us from the primitive harbour of the late 1600s, when large vessels were obliged to anchor in deep water and small boats had to be beached on the shore, to the early 1700s, when a stone quay and gun battery were built, to the 1820s, when a deep-water wharf was constructed to allow ocean-going vessels to load and unload their cargoes directly on the dock.

OVER FIVE HUNDRED ARTEFACTS ON DISPLAY

Exhibits in the lobby show a wide range of artefacts found by archaeologists on the site. In the *Café Artefact* (*preceding pages*) display cases form a timeline, presenting objects that correspond to six phases of the history of the property. Each phase is personified by the name of one of six proprietors who owned the site over the centuries.

The same timeline is reflected in the organization of the six floors of the hotel. Each floor is devoted to a specific period of the history of the property. As in the cross-section of an archaeological dig, the oldest artefacts are displayed on the lower floors and objects dating from more recent periods are displayed on the upper floors. Each hotel room has its own artefact and each room has been given a name inspired by the object displayed within it.

On each floor of the building, display cases beside the elevators present objects dating from the different periods when successive owners

occupied the site – First floor: Charles Aubert de La Chesnaye, 1660-1725; Second floor: Jean Maillou, 1725-1760; Third floor: Hugh Finlay, 1760-1795; Fourth floor: John Chillas, 1795-1825; Fifth floor: the Hunt family, 1825-1880; Sixth floor: The Vallerand Company, 1880-1980.

A NEW LIFE FOR BUILDING MATERIALS FOUND UNDERGROUND

The counters of the reception desks in the lobby are made of oak from 19th-century wharves, also found by the archaeologists. Two entrance pavilions, constructed in 2003, contain stones from masonry structures that were found underground on the site (preceding page, bottom right). An antler is displayed in a niche, by an entrance door leading to the hotel restaurant. The word for antler in French is Panache, and this is the name of the restaurant. In French, as in English, to say that someone has panache means that they have dash and style. The restaurant, located in a former 19th century warehouse, has a special atmosphere that is elegant and contemporary, yet steeped with a sense of history. Massive wooden posts and beams evoke the workaday past of this 19th-century port building (preceding page, top). The metal wheel in the rafters was once used to lift heavy weights with a rope.

IN THE HEART OF THE OLD CITY

The evolution of the site is also expressed in the design of the pavement outside the entrance to the hotel. Paving stones laid in wavy lines on Rue Saint-Antoine show the changing profile of the shoreline over the centuries – in 1600, 1700 and 1800 – as landfill operations were undertaken to enlarge the port area. Historic buildings (facing page), that were integrated into the hotel in 1996, face Rue Saint-Pierre: a 19th-century warehouse residence, adorned with a row of carved stone masks (see also page 105), and the Hunt House.

Three red doors on the facade of Panache restaurant (left) evoke the days when the heavy barrels were transferred from the floors of this former warehouse to tall ships that docked here in the 19th century.

MUSÉE DE LA CIVILISATION

A MODERN INSTITUTION IN AN HISTORIC ENVIRONMENT

T

he *Musée de la civilisation* (Museum of Civilization) is a remarkable example of the successful integration of a modern institution into an historic environment. This great edifice, which opened its doors in 1988, has played a key role in the renaissance of Quebec's lower town, helping to transform a decaying sector, scattered with vacant lots and abandoned buildings, into a thriving neighbourhood, filled with elegant hotels, restaurants, shops and professional offices.

THE ARCHITECTS

The Museum was designed by Moshe Safdie, architect, in partnership with the Montreal architectural firm of Desnoyers Mercure and the Quebec City firm of Belzile, Brassard, Galienne, Lavoie, Sungur Incesulu.

Moshe Safdie was still a young man when he received international recognition for his design of "Habitat 67" for the 1967 Montreal World's Fair. Following this success, he obtained many prestigious contracts in other countries, including the United States and Israel, but none in Canada, until he and his colleagues won the competition for Quebec City's *Musée de la civilisation*. Since that time Moshe Safdie has designed many prestigious buildings around the world, and is now recognized as one of the leading architects of our time.

OLD AND NEW

With its grey limestone walls and steep copper roofs, the museum echoes the architecture of the historic buildings surrounding it, in terms of scale, form, and materials used (*above*). The tower,

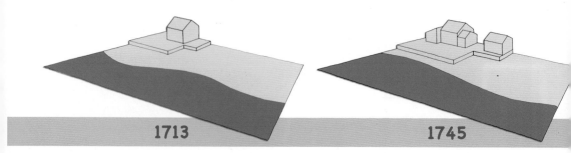

1713

1745

although contemporary in character, evokes the steeples of the churches of the Old City. The central portion of the Museum was designed to be lower than the rest of the edifice, to preserve an impressive view of the cliff and the old Laval University building, with its silver-coloured mansard roof and lantern towers. Staircases allow visitors to cross over the museum's glass-roofed entrance hall to reach *Rue Saint-Pierre*, where they can discover other historic buildings that have been integrated into the museum complex: an 18th-century merchant's house and a 19th-century bank (*see pages 98-99*). In 1985, when construction crews dug beneath the surface of a former parking lot to prepare the site for the future Museum, they uncovered impressive stone walls and docks (*above left*) that had once been part of the 18th and 19th-century port of Quebec. The large stone residence in the background is the *Maison Estèbe*,

built in 1752 and now part of the *Musée de la civilisation* (*above right*). Guillaume Estèbe's arched carriageway originally led from *Rue Saint-Pierre* to a private courtyard and stone dock. A series of diagrams (*below*) shows the evolution of the site over time, as land was reclaimed from the river during the 18th century to create a continuous line of stone docks for Estèbe and other merchants. The last two illustrations clearly indicate the location of the *Maison Estèbe*, both in the 18th century, and today, integrated into the *Musée de la civilisation*. Unfortunately, the construction schedule for the new Museum did not allow enough time for extensive archaeological digs. Nevertheless, thanks to the rapid intervention of conservation specialists, it was possible for vestiges of a long-vanished maritime environment to be integrated into the design of the building.

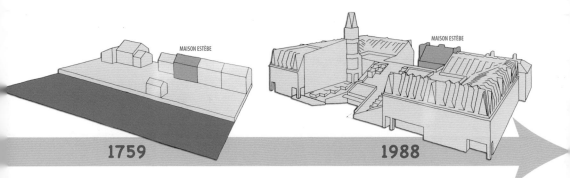

MAISON ESTÈBE

1759

MAISON ESTÈBE

1988

VESTIGES OF A MARITIME ENVIRONMENT

A stone dock has been preserved in the Great Hall (*above*), complete with an iron mooring ring once used by 18th-century sailors to tie up their boats (*below, right*). The hull of a wooden boat (*below, left*), one of eight found underground on the site, is also on display. These boats, which had been abandoned on the beach in the 18th century, were covered over when the shore was filled in behind Guillaume Estèbe's masonry wall, to enlarge his property. In addition to serving as a private dock, this stone structure was designed to protect the merchant's land from the waters of the St. Lawrence at high tide.

Indeed, the St. Lawrence River once flowed where you are standing. A work of art called *La débâcle* evokes the huge pieces of ice that flowed here centuries ago. The French word *débâcle* refers to the spring breakup of the ice. It is interesting to note that, even today, water still infiltrates the ground beneath the Museum. The architects had to design a special waterproof foundation to protect the building from flooding.

A Dynamic Contemporary Museum

The *Musée de la civilisation* presents the history and culture of the province of Quebec, past, present and future, through innovative multi-disciplinary exhibitions. A variety of temporary exhibitions deal with contemporary topics, while three permanent exhibitions provide a broader canvas, introducing visitors to themes that are essential to the Quebec experience: *The People of Quebec...Then and Now* (see the objects displayed on this page), tells the story of life in Quebec from the French Regime to the present day.

Avoiding traditional displays, this contemporary museum borrows from the world of theatre design and other artistic disciplines, to create fascinating environments that present objects in context, focusing on their symbolic value, to help tell a story (*facing page, bottom*).

INTERNATIONAL EXHIBITIONS

In addition to its efforts to help deepen our understanding of the culture and society of the province of Quebec, the museum works in partnership with prestigious institutions in other countries to present major exhibitions of international scope. The exhibition **Rome, From the Origins to Italy's Capital** (*above and facing page, top*), for example, organized by the *Musée de la civilisation* in 2011-2012, involved the participation of over 30 Italian museums.

A MEETING PLACE

A dozen permanent and temporary exhibitions are presented simultaneously at the *Musée de la civilisation*, and an array of lectures, round-table discussions with experts, interactive hands-on workshops and other activities are designed to complement and enhance the visitors' experience. The Great Hall, which serves as a covered public square, provides a meeting space for a wide variety of events. Local citizens' groups are encouraged to gather in the *Musée de la civilisation* to discuss community issues. With a diverse offering of exhibitions and activities to interest people of all ages and backgrounds, the Museum has been highly successful, attracting a vast clientele, both local and international.

PLACE DE LA FAO

FOOD FOR A HUNGRY WORLD

This inspiring monument and public square were inaugurated in 1995 to mark the 50th anniversary of the FAO - the United Nations Food and Agricultural Organization. A bronze plaque to one side honours the memory of Lester B. Pearson, the distinguished Canadian diplomat who played a key role in founding the FAO when the organization was established at a meeting in Quebec City in 1945. Pearson was later awarded the Nobel Peace Prize and went on to become Prime Minister of Canada.

The bronze monument evokes the prow of a sailing ship, with its figurehead in the form of a beautiful woman, her arms laden with food to feed the hungry of the world (*next page*). At the base of the monument, water from a fountain gurgles over imaginary waves of stone that radiate across the square in the pattern of the paving. The wavy lines evoke the vanished shore that once occupied this site. At one time, this was a tidal marshland where the waters of the St. Charles River entered the St. Lawrence. In the early 19th century the shore was covered over by landfill operations to enlarge the lower town.

LAYERS OF MEANING

This remarkable creation, which offers so many layers of meaning, is the work of three sculptors: Richard Purdy, Carmelo Arnoldin and François Hébert, working in partnership with landscape architect André Plante.

A poetic image in low relief at the base of the bronze monument (*next page, bottom right*) depicts an imaginary sailing vessel almost entirely buried beneath *Place de la FAO*, with only its prow and figurehead immerging above the surface.

La Viuriere

HÉBERT PURDY 1993

INSPIRED BY THE BANK OF ENGLAND

The Canadian Imperial Bank of Commerce (below), constructed according to the plans of architect V.D. Horsburgh between 1913 and 1915, has an imposing entrance portico, supported by massive Doric columns. The architect, a Scottish immigrant, took his inspiration from the famous Tivoli Corner in London England (right), designed by Sir John Soane for the Bank of England, between 1803 and 1804. Soane's design was inspired by the Roman Temple of Vesta, constructed during the first century B.C., in Tivoli, Italy.

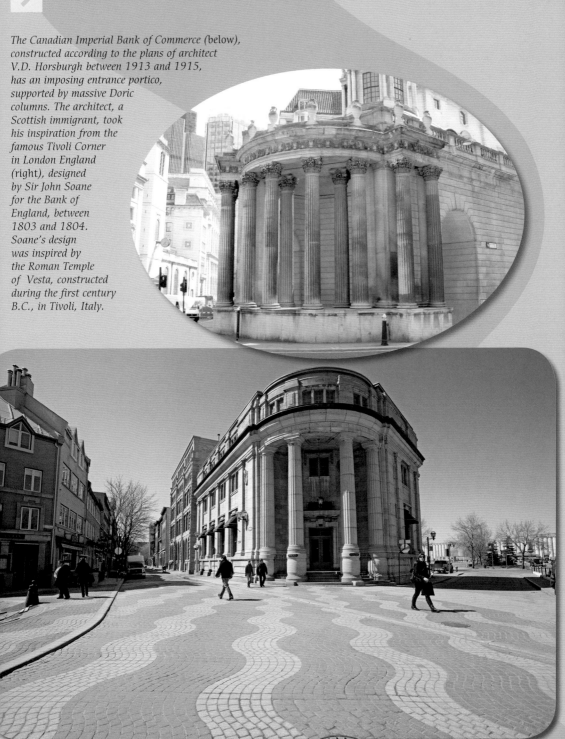

AT THE BASE OF THE CLIFF

A NARROW STRIP OF LAND

During the early days of the French Regime, before landfill operations were undertaken to expand the lower town, the waters of the St. Charles estuary came right up to the base of the cliff at high tide. Passage along the shore thus became very difficult between *Place Royale* and the *Quartier du Palais*, (Palace Quarter) another port area that had developed around the Intendant's Palace during the latter part of the 17th century. Of course, one could always travel from one port sec-tor to the other by boat, but citizens who chose to go by land were obliged to avoid the shoreline altogether when the tide was in; they had to climb the cliff, via the steep *Côte de la Montagne*, cross over the upper town, then descend *Côte du Palais* to finally reach the *Quartier du palais*. By the 1720s, however, a narrow laneway (now called *Rue Sous-le-Cap*) was created along the shoreline to link the two harbour districts. Even then, the lane came to an abrupt end when it reached a small bay at the bottom of the *Côte de la Canoterie*. At that point, people could only continue on to the *Quartier du Palais* at low tide when the water became shallow enough to wade across. The photograph on the previous pages shows the sector on a winter's night, as seen from *Rue des Ramparts* in the upper town. The back stairs, wooden galleries and bridges of the houses in the foreground face narrow *Rue Sous-le-Cap*, at the base of the cliff, while their principal facades face *Rue Saint-Paul*. The upper portions of larger buildings, also facing *Rue Saint-Paul*, dominate the scene: the former Renaud Warehouse, to the left (*see page 110*) and the former Canadian Imperial Bank of Commerce, with its curved entrance façade, facing *Place de la FAO* (*see page 131*), to the right.

RUE SOUS-LE-CAP

Rue Sous-le-Cap or "Street at the Base of the Cliff" is one of the most picturesque lanes in the Old City. In the days of sail, *Rue Sous-le-Cap* was mainly inhabited by coopers who earned their living by making the thousands of barrels required to ship goods in and out of the port of Quebec. A late 19th-century view (*right*) shows wooden bridges that the

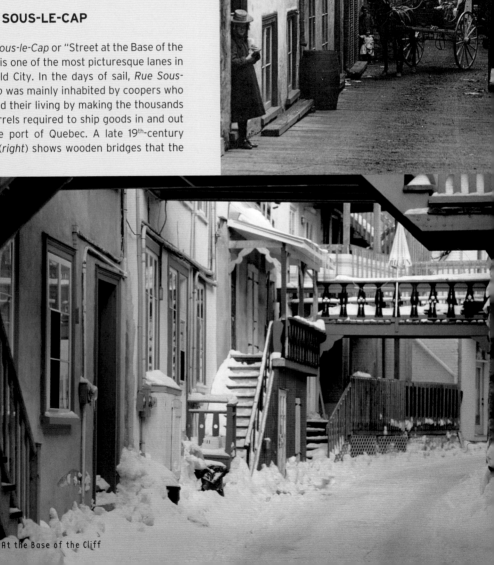

craftsmen built to link their homes with workshops and storage sheds at the base of the cliff. These overhead walkways allowed the artisans and their families to avoid the heavy traffic of horse-drawn vehicles below. Wooden bridges still traverse *Rue Sous-le-Cap* today (*previous page, bottom*), and the narrow lane retains something of the secretive and mysterious atmosphere that has characterized this hidden passageway for centuries.

RUE SAINT-PAUL

By 1817, landfill operations along the shore of the St. Charles River made it possible to open *Rue Saint-Paul*. This wide thoroughfare was a vast improvement over *Rue Sous-le-Cap*, the narrow lane that had been the only means of access between *Place Royale* and the *Quartier du palais* until that time. As the 19th century progressed and the St. Charles estuary became the heart of Quebec's shipbuilding industry, the St-Roch district (west of the *Quartier du palais*), grew by leaps and bounds. The population increased rapidly and the lower town bustled with activity: retail shops began to line the south side of *Rue Saint-Paul*, while on the north side, business owners constructed large edifices, such as the Renaud Warehouse (*see page 110*), and wharves projecting out into the St. Charles River. Starting in the 1860s, a horse-drawn tramway provided transportation along *Rue Saint-Pierre* and *Rue Saint-Paul*, ensuring that these streets became prime locations to establish a shop or business. By the mid-20th century, however, *Rue Saint-Paul* suffered the same fate as the rest of the lower town, as wholesale and retail businesses moved away to the suburbs, seeking better access for vehicles and easier parking. Fortunately the street found new life when antique dealers moved in. Today the locals know it as the *rue des antiquaires* (the antique dealers'street).

Customs House

The Customs House, constructed between 1856 and 1860, originally stood right at the water's edge, with its entrance steps descending directly into the St. Lawrence (*below*). The monumental character of this edifice – with its imposing Doric columns and triangular pediment – made it one of the most prestigious public buildings in the 19th-century port of Quebec. In those days, the duties collected at Customs Houses provided the federal government with most of its revenue. Today the building is quite a distance from the water (*facing page, bottom*). The docks have been extended much further out into the St. Lawrence, to allow the largest cruise ships to dock easily in deep water, even at low tide. The dome and the upper portion of the edifice were modified after two fires damaged the Customs House in 1864 and 1909.

The architect of the Customs House, William Thomas, immigrated to Canada from England in 1843. He became one of the most successful architects in the nation, designing churches, town halls, court houses and market buildings.

Doric columns grace the impressive portico of the Quebec Customs House (*facing page*). The severe classicism of William Thomas's design for the Quebec Customs House is enriched by robust, Italianate details. Stone heads (*above and below*) have been carved into the keystones over the windows. The curious pattern carved in the stone is a type of rustication called vermiculation, described by specialists as "stonework, tooled to imitate worm tracks". William Thomas's sculptural approach to architecture ran in the family. His brother, John Thomas, one of the most respected stone carvers in England, sculpted the intricate Neo-Gothic ornamentation for the tower of Big Ben and the Palace of Westminster, in London.

CREDITS

Concept, text and iconographic research: David Mendel
Photography: Luc-Antoine Couturier
(quebec-photo.com)
Art direction and Graphic design: André Durocher
(syclone.com)
Publisher and Project Coordinator: Sylvain Harvey

English revision: Clive Meredith
French translation: Paule Champoux
Printing: K2 Impressions

Commission de la capitale nationale du Québec
Publishing Director: Denis Angers
Project Coordinator: Hélène Jean
Archivist: Annik Cassista

First edition, 2012
© Éditions Sylvain Harvey and Commission de la
capitale nationale du Québec
ISBN: 978-2-923794-41-9

Printed in Canada

Legal deposit – Bibliothèque et Archives nationales du
Québec, 2012
Legal deposit – Library and Archives Canada, 2012

Éditions Sylvain Harvey
Phone: (418) 692-1336 (Québec City area)
Toll-free: 1 800 476-2068 (Canada and U.S.A.)
E-mail: info@editionssylvainharvey.com
Website: www.editionssylvainharvey.com

Commission de la capitale nationale du Québec
Phone: (418) 528-0773
Toll-free: 1 800 442-0773
E-mail: commission@capitale.gouv.qc.ca
Website: www.capitale.gouv.qc.ca

Distribution in bookstores in Canada
Distribution Ulysse
Phone: (514) 843-9882, extension 2232
Toll-free: 1 800 748-9171
E-mail: info@ulysse.ca

We wish to thank the Société de développement des
entreprises culturelles du Québec (SODEC) for its aid
towards publishing, promotion and translation.

Government of Québec – Tax credit for book publishing
– Administered by SODEC

The publisher wishes to acknowledge the support of
the Canada Council for the Arts through the Book
Publishing Industry Development Program (BPIDP).

This book is also available in French under the title:
Québec, berceau de l'Amérique française
ISBN: 978-2-923794-42-6

ACKNOWLEDGEMENTS

The author and photographer would like to express
their gratitude to all who opened their doors to us,
making accessible many hidden corners of the Old
City: at Parcs Canada, Marie-Josée Bissonnette,
Nicole Ouellet and Mario Demers; at the Archbishop's
Residence, Michel Roberge; at the *SODEC, Direction
du patrimoine immobilier*, Benoit-Pierre Bertrand and
Jean-Louis Simard; at *Notre-Dame-des-Victoires*, Mgr
Denis Bélanger and Francis Jacques; at the *Musée de
la Civilisation*, Serge Poulin and Gaétan Gagner; at the
Auberge St-Antoine, Ingrid Lemm.

Our thanks to the various archivists who provided
access to images from the past, allowing the reader
to travel back in time and see the places of today in a
wider context.

Thanks to those who offered help, information, ideas
and inspiration along the way: Donna McEwen, William
Moss, Allison Bain, Lise Jodoin, Barbara Bignell, Peter
Clibbon and Helen Meredith, with particular thanks to
Clive Meredith, who generously spent many Sunday
afternoons with the author going over the English texts.

Our sincere gratitude to the team whose combined
talent, determination, and effort made it possible to
transform the ephemeral experience of a guided tour
into this book: publisher, Sylvain Harvey; designer,
André Durocher; English revision, Clive Meredith;
translation, Paule Champoux; At the Commission de
la Capitale nationale du Québec: Denis Angers, Hélène
Jean, Annik Cassista.

SOURCES OF ILLUSTRATIONS

P. 8-9 - *A view of Quebec from the South-East*,
engraving, in *Atlantic Neptune*, 1781. Joseph Frederick
Wallet DesBarres, BAnQ Collection Literary and
Historical Society of Quebec.

P. 10. - *Detail of a map of the city of Quebec in 1733*.
Chaussegros de Léry NAC (C -15739).

P. 10-11 - *Quebec from the Micmac Encampment*.
James Pattison Cockburn ROM 955.20.1.

P. 13 - *View of Quebec around 1805*. George Heriot
ROM. (2006_7416._1).

P. 13 - *Passengers and mail crossing the rive*. Cornelius
Krieghoff (lithograph), (ROM 962.156.1).

P. 14-15 - *Old Quebec Quarter-Lower Town around
1880*.Louis-Prudent Vallée, BAnQ, (S6,D1,P432).

P. 16-17 - *Picturesque Canada*, Vol. 1(1882) Private
Collection.

P. 20 - *Old Quebec Quarter – Côte de la Montagne
– Post Office Building, around 1865*. Louis-Prudent
Vallée BAnQ (P546, D3,P41).

P. 36 - *View of the Bishop's Palace and its ruins*. J. Fougeron, after Richard Short, NAC (C-000352).

P. 36-37- *Prescott Gate-Quebec, 1840*. J.Tingle Archives de la Ville de Québec, (negative 10141).

P. 38 - *Côte de la Montagne*, Harper's Weekly, 25 August 1860. P. 38 *A Glimpse from the Old City Wall*. Picturesque Canada Vol. 1 (1882), private collection.

P. 39 - *The Neptune Inn, Quebec, 1830*. James Pattison Cockburn, BAnQ (P600.S5, PIMC32-3).

P. 39 - *Neptune*, Louis Jobin, 1901, Musée national des beaux-arts du Québec

P. 41 - *Breakneck Stairs, Quebec, QC, around 1870*. Louis-Prudent Vallée, McCord Museum (MP-0000.321.2).

P. 50 - *Lower Town Market of Quebec, 1882*. George M. Grant, Greffes et Archives, Ville de Québec (9865).

P. 57 - *Lower Town Church and Market Place, Quebec, around, 1821-1823*. Musée de la Civilisation, Séminaire de Québec (1993.23300).

P. 60 - *Hôtel Louis XIV*, BAnQ (E6, S7, P70037).

P. 62 - *Remains of a tower of Champlain's second Habitation*. Ministère de la culture et des communications, fonds photographique (1976-R-12.8).

P. 66 - *View of the Cathedral Notre Dame de la Victoire*.Richard Short BAC (C-000357).

P. 76 - *The Lower Town Market seen from McCallum's Wharf, Quebec, 4 July 1829*. James Pattison Cockburn BAC (C 150737).

P. 77 - *Finlay Market, around 1860*. Greffes et Archives de la Ville de Québec (9873-1).

P 86 - *French Canadian habitants playing cards, 1848* .Cornelius Krieghoff, BAC (C-000057).

P. 89 - *The Woolsey Family, 1809*.William Berczy, National Gallery of Canada, Ottawa NO. 5875.

P. 91 - Rue Cul de Sac. Barbara H. Stephens, 1929, Collection Barbara Bignell, (Now in the collection of the *Musée des Beaux-Arts de Québec*).

P 92 - *Quebec,Champlain Market, 1907*. Coll. Magella Bureau, BAnQ (P547, S1 SS1, SS1, D001, P3534. VIEW-5684).

P. 94 - *Little Champlain Street, Quebec City*. William Notman & Son, 1916, McCord Museum,VIEW 6586.

P. 100 - *St. Peter Street,Quebec, 1829* James Pattison Cockburn, ROM (951x205.14)

P. 100 - *Rue Saint-Pierre, Québec, QC 1916*. Notman & Son, McCord Museum (VIEW 6586).

P. 103 - *Old Quebec Quarter, Lower Town, Molson Bank, around 1890*. Livernois, BAnQ (P560,S2,D2, P84258-1).

P.106 - *Union Bank, from Quebec Jubilee Illustrated, June 1887*. BAnQ (P600-4,C362-Quebec-1887).

P. 108 - *Withstanding the Attack of Arnold's Men at the Second Barrier*, 1902 .Sydney Adamson BAC (C-005415).

P. 116 - Collection du Laboratoire de Restauration, Université Laval. Padlock (CeET -110 -16D102 -1); Bank token (CeET -110 -11C8 -1); Dominoes (CeEt110-11 C 17-1); Harpoon point (CeEt -110 -1); corkscrew (CeEt -110 -11B20); candle snuffer (CeEt -110 -16K5 -26)

P. 123 - *Photo of the Maison Estèbe and stone remains found below ground*. David Mendel, 1985.

P. 126 - *Skin Talks*. Exhibition, 2002, Musée de la Civilisation

P. 126-127 - Exhibition - Rome, From the Origins to Italy's Capital, 2011-2112, Musée de la Civilisation.

P.131 - *Tivoli Corner, London*. Helen Meredith, 2011.

P 134 - *Rue Sous-le-Cap, Québec, around 1895*. McCord Museum (MP-0000.25.304).

P 136 - *Quebec, the Central Customs House, 1907*. Coll. Magella Bureau BAnQ (P547, S1, SS1, SSS1,D1, P3419).

P.136 - *Customs House*, Picturesque Canada, Vol. 1 (1882) private collection.

FURTHER READING

Some of the publications that deal with the history of the lower town and the city's maritime heritage are: *Quebec* by Marc Vallières, in the *Les régions du Québec, histoire en bref* series (Ste-Foy: Presses de l'Université Laval, 2010); *Quebec, ville et capitale*, under the direction of Serge Courville and Robert Garon, in the *Atlas historique du Québec* series (Ste-Foy: Presses de l'Université Laval, 2001); *Québec, ville maritime*, Continuité, numéro 116, printemps 2008; *Québec fleuron du patrimoine mondial*, (Québec: Cap-aux-Diamants, Édition spéciale, 1987); *Vieux-Québec Cap-Blanc, Place forte et port de mer*, by Danielle Blanchet, Louise Forget and Sylvie Thivierge (Québec: Ville de Québec, 1989); *Le Saint-Laurent et les Grands Lacs au temps de la voile, 1608-1850*, by Pierre Camu (Lasalle: Éditions Hurtubise, 1996); *Le Saint Laurent et ses Pilotes, 1805-1860*, by Jean Leclerc (Montreal: Leméac,1990). Among the publications dealing with specific sites and monuments are: *Place-Royale, Quatre siècles d'histoire*, by René Côté (Québec: Fides, Musée de la Civilisation, 2000); on the Laval Monument: *Founding Fathers, The Celebration of Champlain and Laval in the Streets of Quebec, 1878-1908*, by Donald Rudin (Toronto: University of Toronto Press, 2003); *Les escaliers public en fer de la ville de Québec, Entre fonctionnalité et représentation, 1880-1900*, by Marie-Eve Bonenfant (Ste-Foy: Septentrion, 2006); *Le Rêve du Petit Champlain, Vieux-Québec 1976-1985*, by Jacques de Blois (Sillery: Septentrion, 2007); on the Auberge St-Antoine: *Un passé plus-que-parfait*, by Camille Lapointe (Quebec: Les Éditions Sylvain Harvey, 2007); Other publications that deal with archaeology in the lower town are: *Dreams of the Americas: Overview of New France Archaeology*, under the direction of Christian Roy and Hélène Côté (Québec, Archéologique, Collection Hors Série 2, 2008; *The Recent Archaeology of the Early Modern Period in Quebec City*, Guest Editor William Moss, Post-Medieval Archaeology, Vol. 43, Part 1, 2009.